Three-dimensional structure of wood

Three-dimensional structure of wood

AN ULTRASTRUCTURAL APPROACH

B. G. BUTTERFIELD

Botany Department
University of Canterbury
Christchurch, New Zealand

and

B. A. MEYLAN

Physics and Engineering Laboratory
Department of Scientific and Industrial Research
Lower Hutt, New Zealand

SECOND EDITION

1980
LONDON   NEW YORK
CHAPMAN AND HALL
150TH ANNIVERSARY

Preface

Nine years ago saw the publication of the first version of *Three-dimensional Structure of Wood: A scanning electron microscope study* [95]. This book contained 59 scanning electron micrographs and a modest text outlining the basic structure of wood. When we wrote it in 1970, the scanning electron microscope was still something of a novelty (the first commercially produced SEM only coming on the market in 1965) and its use as an instrument in serious wood research was still treated by many with a good deal of suspicion. Such suspicions were not without foundation for indeed the first *Three-dimensional Structure of Wood* was put together from a somewhat paltry collection of a few hundred scanning electron micrographs of wood taken over a two year period.

The last decade has seen some remarkable developments in the general understanding of the structure of wood. Our personal collection of scanning electron micrographs has grown from a few hundred to some 16 000. Techniques for specimen preparation [46, 47], particularly in the areas of dehydration [36] and coating have greatly improved. Most significant however, has been the new depth of understanding of wood ultrastructure that has become almost universal. By combining the use of the light, transmission and scanning electron microscopes, scientists in many widely separated parts of the world have now added a vast amount of information to our understanding of such aspects of wood structure as perforation plate development, tylose formation, the formation of reaction wood, septate fibres ultrastructure, etc. With *Three-dimensional Structure of Wood* now out-of-print in most of its imprints, the time has clearly come for an updated successor to appear. This new *Three-dimensional Structure of Wood* retains almost nothing of the old except its title. It has been written without reference to its out-of-print predecessor. It is, in effect, a completely new book. As such it combines the best illustrative micrographs of various wood anatomical features that we have been able to achieve to date, with the current theories on wood structure and function. For the post-graduate student and research scientist, many text statements are supported by reference to the original publications listed in Section 5. With the exception of certain older major review articles, only publications from 1970 onwards are cited. In most cases, reference to these will put the reader in contact with the older literature for each field.

Like its predecessor the new *Three-dimensional Structure of Wood* is intended primarily as a teaching aid for botany and forestry students of universities, forestry institutes and technical colleges. (For this purpose sets of 35 mm transparencies of many of the figures in this book are also available from the publisher.) However, we hope that it will also find its way onto the bookshelves of many wood research scientists as a source of additional information on the complexity and variability of one of the world's most important renewable resources.

We are again particularly indebted to Mr R. R. Exley who has provided technical assistance over the years that we have worked together. The electron micrographs were taken on the Cambridge scanning electron microscope of the Physics and Engineering Laboratory, DSIR, Lower Hutt, New Zealand. We would also like to express our thanks to Dr J. F. Levy of the Botany Department, Imperial College of Science and Technology, London, for kindly reading the manuscript and offering helpful advice and criticism.

Some of the micrographs in this book have previously been published in some of our research papers and our book *The Structure of New Zealand Woods* [104]. Permission to reproduce them has been kindly given by the editors of the following journals:

Australian Journal of Botany, (1972) **20**, 79 – 86, Figs. 139, 150; **20**, 253 – 9, Figs. 149, 151 and 154.

International Association of Wood Anatomists Bulletin, (1972/1) 3 – 9, Fig. 40; (1972/4) 3 – 9, Fig. 14; (1974/1) 10 – 15, Figs. 26 and 27; (1975/3) 39 – 42, Fig. 144.

New Phytologist, (1978) **81**, 139 – 46, Figs. 28, 29, 31, 34, 36 and 37.

New Zealand DSIR Bulletin, 222 Structure of New Zealand Woods, (1978) Figs. 7, 20, 21, 167, 170, 172 and 176.

New Zealand Journal of Botany, (1972) **10**, 437 – 46, Fig. 190; (1974) **12**, 3 – 18, Figs. 22, 23, 24, 25 and 27; (1975) **13**, 1 – 18, Figs. 145, 146, 147 and 155; (1976) **14**, 123 – 30, Figs. 174, 176 and 177.

Wood Science and Technology, (1978) **13**, 59 – 65, Fig. 41.

First published 1972
Second edition 1980

Published by Chapman and Hall Ltd,
11 New Fetter Lane, London EC4P 4EE

Published in the U.S.A. by
Chapman and Hall
in association with Methuen, Inc.,
733 Third Avenue, New York NY 10017

Typeset by Scarborough Typesetting Services
and printed in Great Britain by
Shenval Press Ltd, London and Harlow

ISBN 0 412 16320 9

British Library Cataloguing in Publication Data

Meylan, Brian Augustus
    Three-dimensional structure of wood. – 2nd ed.

    1. Wood – Anatomy – Atlases
    I. Title   II. Butterfield, Brian Geoffrey
    674′ .12   QK647   80–49953

    ISBN 0–412–16320–9

Contents

1 The Structure of wood

Wood is a complex biological material, known also as *secondary xylem*. It is derived from the vascular cambium and develops in the stems and roots of most gymnosperms and many angiosperms as a consequence of secondary growth [141]. It consists largely of an assemblage of thickened cell walls deposited by the cell cytoplasm during differentiation. In most cells the cytoplasm then dies leaving them devoid of any living contents.

(a) *Softwoods and hardwoods*

Woods are usually divided into two main groups, the *softwoods* and the *hardwoods*. These terms derive from the medieval timber trade. The woods of the gymnosperms are referred to as softwoods and they are formed predominantly of tracheids with only a small amount of parenchyma present. The woods of the pines, spruces and firs, therefore, are more uniform in texture and as a consequence are relatively easy to work. Angiosperm dicotyledonous woods on the other hand, contain a greater variety of cell types, including thick-walled fibres. They are sometimes difficult to work and so the term hardwood has been traditionally used in the timber trade. These terms, however, are rather misleading as hard and soft textured woods can be found in both groups of plants. Balsa wood (*Ochroma* sp), for example, although texturally very soft is an angiosperm and therefore a hardwood by definition. The specific gravity of xylem wall material is more or less constant in all woody plants. Thus the density and hardness of a particular wood is largely governed by the proportion of thick walled cells present. Balsa wood contains a large proportion of thin walled parenchyma cells and is therefore very light. Other plants may have a high proportion of thick walled cells and their wood is accordingly much heavier and harder.

(b) *Cellular nature of wood*

Unlike most plant ground tissue (pith, cortex, etc.) where the cells are more or less isodiametric, the cells of wood are usually elongate structures. This is a necessary development for good conduction and along-the-stem strength. All wood cell types are, therefore, arranged into 'along-the-axis' (termed *axial*) or 'across-the-axis' (termed *radial*) systems. For this reason it is usually easier to examine the cellular structure of wood if it is cut across the axial (termed *transverse*) and along the axial (termed *longitudinal*) planes (Fig. 1). These basic planes of orientation are used both when preparing thin sections of wood for optical microscopy and when making surface cuts of wood blocks for scanning electron microscopy. Throughout this book the abbreviations TF, TLF, and RLF are used to indicate the transverse face, the tangential longitudinal face and the radial longitudinal face respectively of the cut cube of wood.

Most conducting or tracheary cells (tracheids and vessel elements), and support cells (tracheids and fibres), run axially along the stem or root. Ribbons of parenchyma cells termed *rays* run radially from the stem centre outwards to the vascular cambium. The percentage of ray tissue to axial tissue in any wood is best determined from tangential longitudinal sections or faces.

(c) *Growth rings*

Most woody plants grow periodically rather than continuously. This is true of both the apical or vertical growth of the shoot and the radial or lateral growth of the individual stem. In temperate climates such periodicity can be correlated with the change in seasons, growth being most active during the spring and summer months, then passing through a period of partial or total dormancy during the colder winter months. In tropical regions growth may be continuous or intermittent and cannot be as easily correlated with seasonal changes in environment as in temperate regions.

The seasonal pattern of growth in temperate trees is reflected in the formation of a series of *growth increments* or *growth rings* in the wood [42]. These are visible in cut transverse and radial longitudinal faces (Figs. 1, 55 – 60, 132 and 133). In temperate zones these growth rings are produced one per year and are referred to as *annual rings*. They are discernible to the naked eye in cross section because of changes in the size and shape of the cells and the thickness of their cell walls within the growth ring. Where the growth rings are annual it is possible to determine the age of the stem at that height by counting the number of growth increments between the stem centre and the vascular cambium.

Not all growth increments are necessarily annual. Even in trees grown in temperate zones minor climatic changes, such as temperature changes and periods of drought can cause a reduction or cessation of cambial activity. This can result in the formation of *false rings*. Additionally, because the cambial stimulus spreads basipetally down the tree, a growth ring present at an upper level in the trunk may be much narrower or even totally absent at a lower level. Some trees are characterized by partial growth rings, called *lenses*, where the vascular cambium has been active around only part of its circumference during a period of growth.

In tropical climates, where environmental conditions

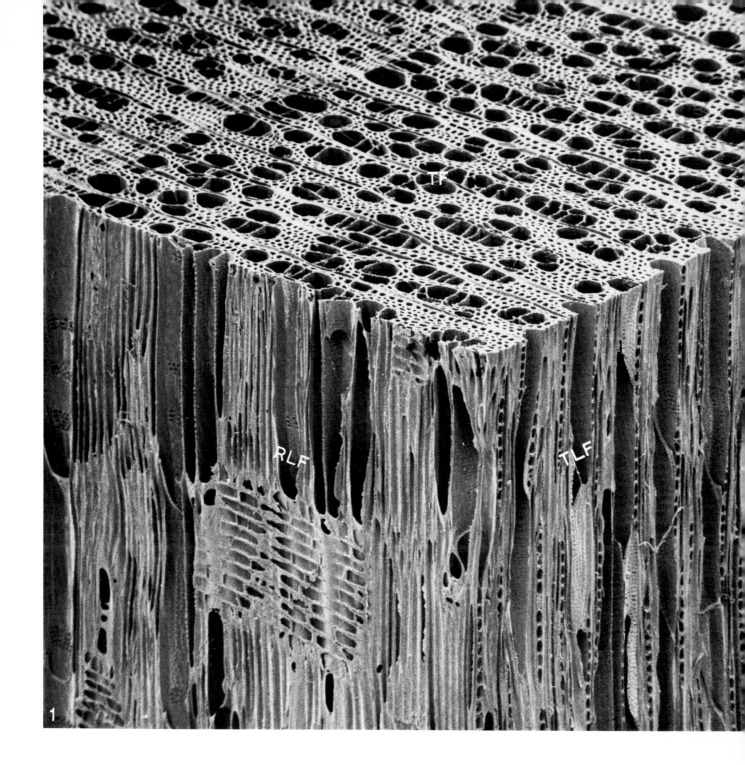

Fig. 1. The wood of the evergreen angiosperm (hardwood) tree *Nothofagus solandri* var. *cliffortioides* (Col.) Ckn. (Fagaceae). The three basic planes *transverse* (TF), *tangential longitudinal* (TLF) and *radial longitudinal* (RLF) are indicated. The relationship between the axial elements (vessels (V) and fibres (F)) and the ray elements (ray parenchyma (R)) can be best understood by examining each of these three planes or cut faces separately and in various combinations. Because of the technical difficulties involved in cutting cleanly the three faces on the one wood specimen it is not realistic to expect to examine these faces simultaneously in many wood samples. TF/TLF/RLF × 140.

are less limiting, the growing season tends to be longer than in temperate regions. Even when conditions are ideal, however, growth is not always continuous. In tropical woods the growth increments are induced by the alternation of wet and dry seasons rather than by an annual period of dormancy. As a consequence, several growth rings may represent one calendar year under these conditions. Under uniform growing conditions, growth rings may be completely absent.

Where the growth rings are annual rings, the cells formed in the early period of active growth constitute the *earlywood* or *springwood*, while those cells laid down by the cambium towards the end of the growing season, form the *latewood* or *summerwood*. The demarcation line between latewood and earlywood is termed the *growth ring boundary*. The severity of this boundary depends on the degree of difference between the latewood cells of one ring and the earlywood cells of the next. Softwood tracheids show differences in their cell wall thickness and lumen diameter across a growth ring boundary (Fig. 55). Hardwood fibres may show the same differences (Fig. 169). The greater variety of cell types in hardwoods, however, allows for a much greater variation in cell distribution within the growth ring than is possible in softwoods. As a consequence hardwood growth ring boundaries may be marked by differences in the types of cell present as well as differences in wall thickness and lumen diameter of individual cells (*see* Section 4.1). The study of growth rings forms the very extensive science of *dendrochronology*.

(d) Sapwood – heartwood

Cross sections through the entire trunk of some trees may show a distinct colour change between the dark coloured central *heartwood* zone of the stem and the lighter coloured and more peripheral *sapwood* region. The proportion of the stem radius occupied by heartwood varies with the age of the stem. Generally, the greater bulk of the stemwood is sapwood in young trees but with increasing age the heartwood may occupy an ever increasing fraction of the stem radius such that in old trees the sapwood may constitute merely a narrow peripheral zone beneath the bark.

Although colour is used as an indicator of the heartwood – sapwood boundary, its use is not strictly correct in terms of the true definitions of heartwood and sapwood. Sapwood is secondary xylem where the tracheary cells are active in conduction and the physiological activities of the wood are performed by living axial and ray parenchyma cells and fibres. The transition to heartwood is marked by the deposition of extractives and other extraneous materials in the cells, and in the case of some hardwoods, by the accelerated production of tyloses. The death of all living cells then follows [6] so that heartwood is a physiologically dead tissue.

Although the corewood of many trees is technically heartwood, it may not show any colour difference from the sapwood.

1.1 The cell wall

The walls of wood cells consist largely of three substances, cellulose, lignin and hemicellulose. The cellulose is in the form of extremely long crystalline microfibrils of great tensile strength and often termed the framework component. These microfibrils are embedded in and bound together by the lignin and hemicellulose – often called the encrusting components or matrix. The wall structure thus forms a natural fibre-composite but differs from artificial composite materials in that the matrix is water reactive and changes both its volume and elastic properties with moisture content [53, 142].

Cell walls are subdivided into primary walls [73] and secondary walls according to their time of formation. The primary wall develops first and is often stretched during the differentiation of the cell. It is the only wall found in some cells (e.g. some ray parenchyma cells). The secondary wall is laid down on the inside of the primary wall, usually after elongation of the cell has ceased. It is a characteristic feature of almost all wood cells and is usually considerably thicker than the primary wall.

There is a most extensive literature on the structure of the tracheid and fibre cell wall, no doubt because of their importance in the pulp and paper and other industries. The primary wall consists of a thin network of irregularly arranged microfibrils. In the secondary wall three layers designated S_1, S_2, and S_3 can usually be distinguished (Fig. 62), each having a different helical arrangement of its microfibrils (Fig. 2). The layer nearest the primary wall is termed the S_1 layer and the microfibrils in it are orientated nearly perpendicular to the long side of the cell. The middle, or S_2 layer is the thickest and is built up of microfibrils running at a small angle to the long axis of the cell. The S_3 layer, lying nearest to the cell lumen, is a thin layer with the microfibrils again orientated in a nearly transverse direction. There may be a gradual transition in microfibril orientation from one layer to the next. The S_3 layer is occasionally overlaid, inside the cell lumen, by a covering termed the warty layer.

Each of the three secondary wall layers is believed to consist of alternate lamellae of polysaccharide and lignin [121, 144]. Each polysaccharide lamella consists of a single layer of parallel microfibrils of cellulose sheathed in a monomolecular layer of hemicelluloses. In the S_2 layer at least, these lamellae are interrupted and are not continuous right around the cell wall [144].

The wall structure in other xylem cells is not so clearly understood. Some parenchyma cells appear to have a

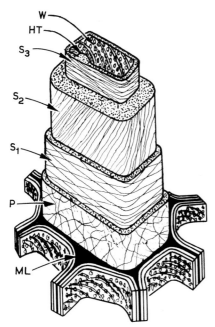

Fig. 2. A schematic diagram to illustrate the general structure of the cell wall of axially elongated wood elements and the dominant, helical orientation of the cellulose microfibrils within each wall layer. ML, middle lamella; P, primary wall, S_1, outer layer of the secondary wall, S_2, middle layer of the secondary wall; S_3, innermost layer of the secondary wall; HT, helical thickening; W, warty layer.

three layered wall structure similar to that of fibres but others have a quite dissimilar crossed polylaminate structure [31, 34]. Vessel element walls have a wide range of structures [79, 80]. Some are three layered like fibres, though with relatively thick S_1 and S_3 layers, others have a single secondary wall layer with a relatively uniform flat helix; and yet others have a complex multi-layered structure. It should be noted that in the vicinity of pits the microfibril orientation can be considerably disturbed.

After secondary wall deposition is complete, a further layer known as the *tertiary wall layer* may form over the lumen surface. Tertiary walls are known to occur in the ray and axial parenchyma cells [32], vessels [21, 114], and fibres (*see* Section 4.5) of various woods. When present in vessel associated ray and axial parenchyma cells they are termed the *protective layer* and sometimes play a role in tylose formation.

The warty layer is believed to consist largely of a lignin-like material together with an amorphous carbo-hydrate [2, 4]. Warts are present in almost all conifer tracheids [86, 113], and also in *Gnetum* [151]. In the angiosperms, vessels, tracheids and fibres may all be warted but there is a tendency for warts to be absent from the vessels and libriform fibres of advanced woods [129].

Warts develop external to the plasma membrane after the microfibrils of the innermost secondary wall layer have been deposited and the greater part of wall lignifi-cation is completed [3, 171]. They may be deposited over normal wall surfaces, helical thickenings, perforation plate borders and inside pit chambers (Fig. 9). They can develop either internal to the S_3 layer (Figs. 63, 78 and 82), or in compression wood tracheids, internal to the S_2 layer (Fig. 102).

Individual cells are joined together by intercellular material between their primary walls. This middle lamella is an amorphous mass, rich in lignin and low in cellulose, composed largely of pectin compounds. It is readily dissolved away by macerating solutions.

1.2 Cell wall pitting

The secondary walls of wood cells show characteristic openings or depressions termed *pits*. Pits are gaps in the secondary wall forming a canal between the cell lumen and the primary wall. The pits of two contiguous cells usually oppose one another to form a *pit-pair*. The primary walls of the two such opposing cells, and the intervening middle lamella, form what is termed the *pit membrane*. The presence of this dividing structure distinguishes a pit from a *perforation* where there is a complete opening from one cell to another.

Pits arise during the ontogeny of the cell wall [9, 69, 156]. Areas of the primary walls are modified by the presence of plasmodesmata and, in vessel elements and conifer tracheids and possibly in other cell types, the microfibrils in the area of the pit are deposited in a pattern that differs from the normal reticulate texture of the primary wall. The secondary wall is then deposited over the primary wall except for the immediate vicinity of these modified areas. Where a canal through the secondary wall is of similar diameter to the pit mem-brane, the opening is said to be a *simple pit* (Fig. 3a). Where the secondary wall overarches the pit membrane leaving an aperture that is smaller than the membrane itself, the structure is termed a *bordered pit* (Fig. 3b) and the enclosed cavity is termed the *pit chamber*. Bordered pits have the advantage of producing a large area of pit membrane with a minimum loss of strength by inter-ruption of the cell wall. Where the opposing pits in the walls of two contiguous cells are both simple they form a *simple pit-pair*. Where they are both bordered they form a *bordered pit-pair* and when one pit is bordered and the other is simple, they form a *half-bordered pit-pair* (Figs. 3c and 18). Sometimes several small pits in the wall of one cell may oppose a single larger pit in the wall of a contiguous cell. Such an arrangement is known as *unilateral compound pitting*. If a pit does not exactly oppose another in a neighbouring cell or if it abuts an inter-cellular space then it forms a *blind pit* (Figs. 3d and 82).

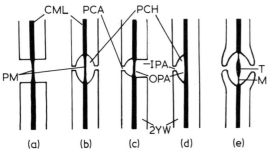

Fig. 3. Diagrammatic representation of various types of pits and pit-pairs between contiguous cells as seen in longitudinal section: (a) two simple pits forming a simple pit-pair; (b) two bordered pits forming a bordered pit-pair; (c) a bordered pit opposing a simple pit in a contiguous cell forming a half bordered pit-pair; (d) a simple pit not matched in a contiguous cell and forming a blind pit; (e) a conifer bordered pit. Abbreviations: PM – pit membrane, T – torus, M – margo, PCH – pit chamber, PCA – pit canal, IPA – inner pit aperture, OPA – outer pit aperture, CML – compound middle lamellae, and 2YW – secondary wall.

1.2.1. *Bordered pits*

Bordered pits are found in the walls of hardwood vessels and vascular tracheids, the fibres of certain woods and in a more specialized form in the walls of conifer tracheids [8, 49] (Fig. 3e).

In the earlywood tracheids of most conifers the secondary wall is raised to form a border [61] that over-arches the pit membrane and pit chamber (Fig. 4). The pit membrane is circular in outline and modified into two zones: a centrally thickened *torus*, often heavily encrusted, suspended by a *margo* of cellulose microfibrils (Fig. 5). Some of these microfibrils are aligned radially and others more randomly. The radial arrangements tend to show up more prominently in less critically prepared wood samples presumably due to the collapse of the finer network during sample preparation (Fig. 7). The open nature of the margo results from the removal of the non-cellulosic components of the primary walls and middle lamella [70, 128, 157]. A direct pathway for sap exists, therefore, from one tracheid to another through the margo and pit apertures of the two opposing pits. Under certain conditions of stress [14, 87, 140], such as embolism or drying [13, 58], the conifer tracheid pit membrane deflects to one side or the other of the pit chamber so that the torus obstructs the pit aperture and effectively seals the pit-pair [41]. In this condition the pit-pair is said to be *aspirated* (Figs. 7 and 8). Pit aspiration is an irreversible process. It is made possible by the extension of the microfibrillar net of the margo and occurs as a natural phenomenon in heartwood and also, at sites of injury, in the sapwood. Pit aspiration increases the resistance of timber to the impregnation of preservatives.

Fig. 4. Conifer bordered pits in the radial walls of earlywood tracheids in *Pinus radiata* D. Don (Pinaceae). Water ascending the trunk of the living tree passes from one tracheid to the next through the pit aperture of one cell, into the pit chamber, through the pit membrane which remains suspended in a middle position and into the pit chamber of the second cell and finally out into the second tracheid. TF/TLF × 1250.

Fig. 5. Conifer bordered pit-pair membrane in *Libocedrus plumosa* (Don) Sargent (Cupressaceae) exposed by removing the cell wall of the contiguous tracheid. Note the centrally thickened torus and the more open margo. RLF Split wall × 5500.

Fig. 6. Exposed thick latewood pit membrane in *Pinus radiata* lacking any obvious pores in the margo (the tear across the bottom is a preparation artifact). The absence of pores in the margo is sometimes due to the reticulate network of microfibrils remaining unseparated but can result from the secondary deposition of encrusting materials. RLF Split wall × 7250.

Fig. 7. An aspirated conifer pit membrane in *Podocarpus ferrugineus* G. Benn. ex Don (Podocarpaceae). The pit membrane has deflected away from the reader to lie against the pit chamber wall of the opposing tracheid. The torus has now effectively blocked the pit aperture of the farther tracheid. After aspiration, many of the microfibrils of the margo frequently display a more definite radial alignment. Some thicker macrofibrils, presumably formed from aggregations of radially stretched microfibrils, may also appear. RLF Split wall × 6000.

Fig. 8. Longitudinal cut through the radial walls of two contiguous tracheids in *Pinus radiata* D. Don (Pinaceae). The pit membrane in the pit-pair can be clearly seen aspirated against the pit aperture of the left hand tracheid. TLF × 4000.

Fig. 9. A warty layer lining the pit chamber of a tracheid bordered pit in *Cupressus macrocarpa* Gord. (Cupressaceae). RLF Split wall × 7000.

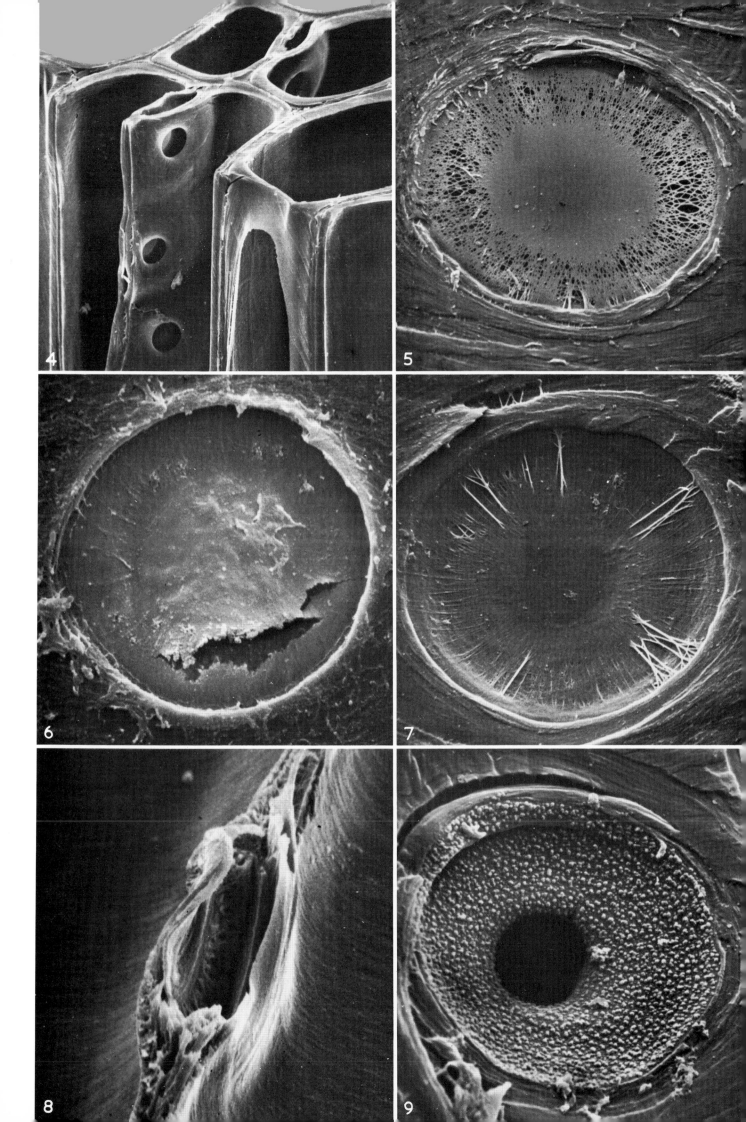

It is not uncommon to find the pit borders lined with warts inside the pit chamber (Fig. 9).

Differences in the morphology of the conifer pit membrane are evident between earlywood and latewood tracheids, and also between woods of different genera [8, 10, 108]. The tracheids occurring in conifer latewood do not usually have specialized 'conifer bordered pits'. Instead the pits tend to be smaller with elliptical (Fig. 62) rather than circular apertures and usually lack the raised border characteristic of the earlywood cells. Although the pits are still bordered, the pit chamber is smaller and the pit membrane sometimes lacks a distinct margo and torus. These differences are in keeping with the transition in main function from conduction in early-wood to support in latewood. The small interruption to the cell wall by the pits in the latewood tracheids decreases their strength less and the absence of a margo in the pit membrane is in keeping with the cells lesser role in conduction.

Reduced bordered pits with pit membranes lacking a torus are also a feature of hardwood fibre-tracheids (Fig. 10). The pit is still divided into a pit chamber and pit canal, but the latter is often quite long forming an inner pit aperture on the lumen end and an outer pit aperture on the pit chamber end. If the size of the inner (lumen) aperture is greater than the outer (chamber) aperture, the pit is said to be *extended* (Fig. 11) and if the reverse is true it is said to be *included*. When the inner aperture is extended, the opening is commonly elliptical or slit shaped. The long axes of the apertures tend to follow the angle of the S_2 microfibrils (Fig. 12). The long axes of the inner pit apertures of a pit-pair connecting two contiguous fibres, therefore, normally form a *crossed pit-pair*.

Bordered pits also occur in the walls of hardwood vessels [19] (Fig. 13). Although the secondary wall over-arches the pit membrane forming a pit chamber, the canal is usually very short and often quite wide. The pit membrane usually is of uniform thickness and frequently shows a microfibrillar texture (Fig. 14). Pit membranes with a torus have been reported in some hardwoods [119]. Branched pits are formed as successive wall layers are added and the pit apertures of two or more adjacent pit canals are brought gradually closer together forming a single pit cavity. This usually occurs only in fibres but the coalescence of close pits can also occur in vessel walls (Fig. 15).

1.2.2 *Simple pits*

Simple pits, by definition lack a border and have a pit canal that is approximately uniform in shape with only minor changes from the pit membrane to the lumen aperture. They occur in libriform fibres (Fig. 16) where they frequently have extended inner apertures. Most axial and ray parenchyma cell pits are also simple (Fig.

Fig. 10. Transverse cut through a reduced bordered pit-pair between two contiguous fibre tracheids in *Griselinia littoralis* Raoul. (Griseliniaceae). Note the long pit canals, the small pit chamber and the thin pit membrane. TF × 9000.

Fig. 11. Extended pits in the fibre walls in *Magnolia grandiflora* L. (Magnoliaceae). In an extended pit, the inner (lumen) aperture (IA) is larger than the outer (pit membrane) aperture (OA). Note the coalescence of the two pit apertures in the lower right of the micrograph. RLF × 2300.

Fig. 12. Bordered pits in the fibres of *Archeria traversii* Hook.f. (Epacridaceae) with extended inner apertures. The long axes of the pit apertures approximately follow the angle of the S_2 layer microfibrils. RLF × 1150.

Fig. 13. Intervessel bordered pit-pairs in *Beilschmedia tawa* (A. Cunn.) Benth. (Lauraceae). Again note the pit canals, the small pit chambers and the thin membranes. RLF × 4100.

Fig. 14. Surface view of the intervessel bordered pit membranes in *Knightia excelsa* R.Br. (Proteaceae) exposed by separating two contiguous cells. In this micrograph the microfibrils of the pit membranes lie in a reticulate arrangement near the centre of each pit membrane and in a circumferential orientation near the periphery. RLF Split wall × 8500.

Fig. 15. The coalescence of the inner pit apertures in the vessel walls of *Tectona grandis* L.f. (Verbenaceae) forming branched pits. RLF × 2000.

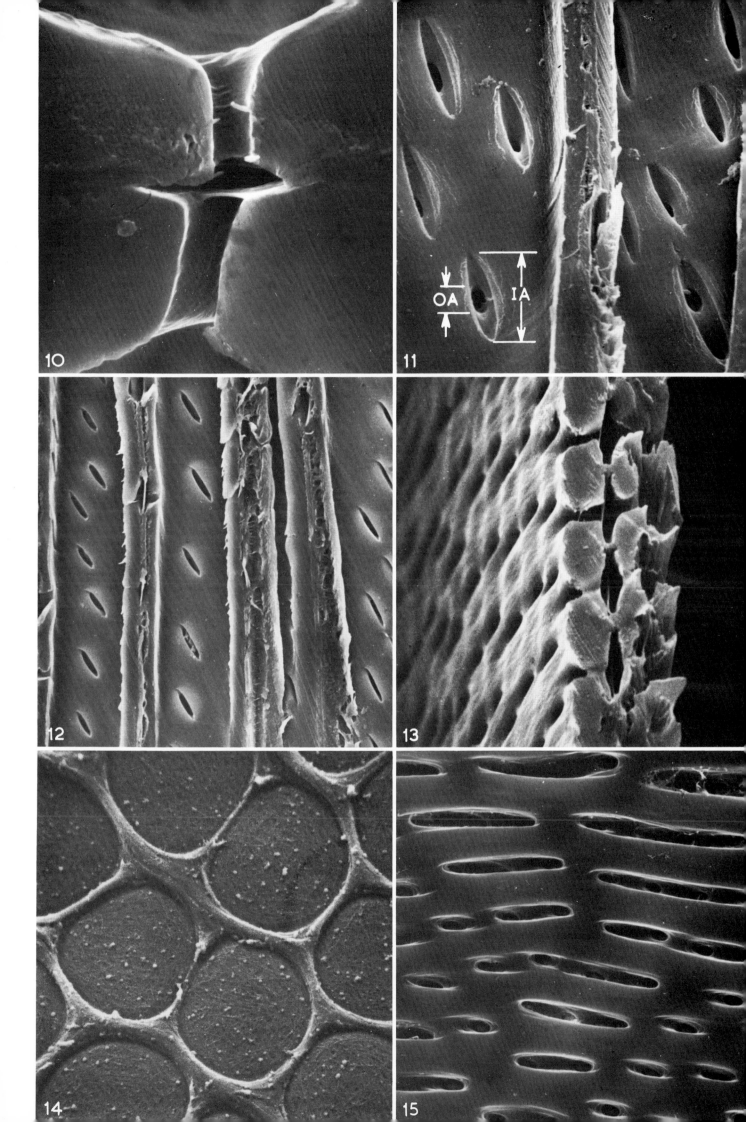

17), but in ray parenchyma cells in particular, the wall may be so thin that a pit canal as such is virtually non-existent (Figs. 18 and 60). Some authors consider these to be blind pits [89].

As in the bordered pit, the pit membrane of the simple pit is composed of the primary walls and middle lamella of the adjacent cells.

1.2.3 *Vestured pits*

Vestures are outgrowths or deposits in the pit chambers and apertures of tracheid [50], vessel element and fibre bordered pits. They are known to occur as normal structures in almost all of the woods of some dicotyledonous families and in some woods of other families [90]. They also occur in *Gnetum* [125, 151]. They are most common in the intervessel pits [100] (Figs. 19, 22–26, 163 and 164), but may also occur in vessel to axial parenchyma and vessel to ray parenchyma pits (Fig. 20). They also occur occasionally in fibre pits [23, 100, 151] (Figs. 21 and 27), but are only rarely a feature of parenchyma cells or tracheids.

Vestures are formed after the completion of cell wall deposition and can be distinguished from the cell wall by their different density and non-fibrillar nature [146]. It has been suggested that they are formed by the prolongation of the activity of the protoplast in the pit as the cell dies. They closely resemble the particles of the warty layer [151, 168, 170] (Fig. 23), but are generally larger and more complex. It is frequently impossible to distinguish between the two on either morphological or chemical grounds [150]. This is particularly evident where the vestures spread out of the pit aperture on the lumen wall (Fig. 22). This similarity in appearance has led to speculation that vestures and warts have a common origin [38]. Alternatively it has often been suggested that vestures are formed by a living cytoplasm whereas warts may be remnants of the dead protoplast [146].

The location, size and shape of the vestures are frequently characteristic of a particular wood [116]. They normally line the pit aperture (Fig. 24), but may spread well beyond this area [23, 116, 180]. In many woods they line the wall of the pit chamber as well (Figs. 19 and 25) and also spread out on the lumen wall of the vessel or fibre [23, 100, 116] (Figs. 26, 27 and 164). Their size and shape also vary [71]. Individual vestures may be branched or unbranched [38], and filamentous, bead-like, coralloid, or foliate in shape [78]. They may also be classified according to their point of attachment into: Type A, where the vestures are attached to all parts of the pit chamber wall and branch into a mass of vestures of equal thickness; Type B, where the vestures are attached to the pit chamber wall close to the pit canal and branch to various extents into thinner vestures [166]. Although various attempts have been made to

Fig. 16. A simple pit-pair between two fibres in *Aralidium pinnatifidum* Bl. (Araliaceae Taxonomy under review). Microfibrillar material is sometimes present in the narrow pit canals of libriform fibres. TF × 5500.

Fig. 17. Simple pits in the axial parenchyma cells of *Knightia excelsa* R.Br. (Proteaceae). Bordered pits can be seen in the vessel wall to the left and slit extended fibre pits in the fibre to the right. RLF × 1100.

Fig. 18. Simple pits in the ray cells of *Pinus radiata* D. Don (Pinaceae). These pits form half-bordered pit pairs with the adjacent tracheid pits. TF × 2200.

Fig. 19. Vestures lining the pit chambers of the intervessel pits in *Eugenia maire* A. Cunn. (Myrtaceae). RLF × 6500.

Fig. 20. Part-vestured vessel to ray pits in *Eugenia maire*. RLF × 900.

Fig. 21. Vestured fibre pits in *Metrosideros excelsa* Sol. ex Gaertn. (Myrtaceae). RLF × 2900.

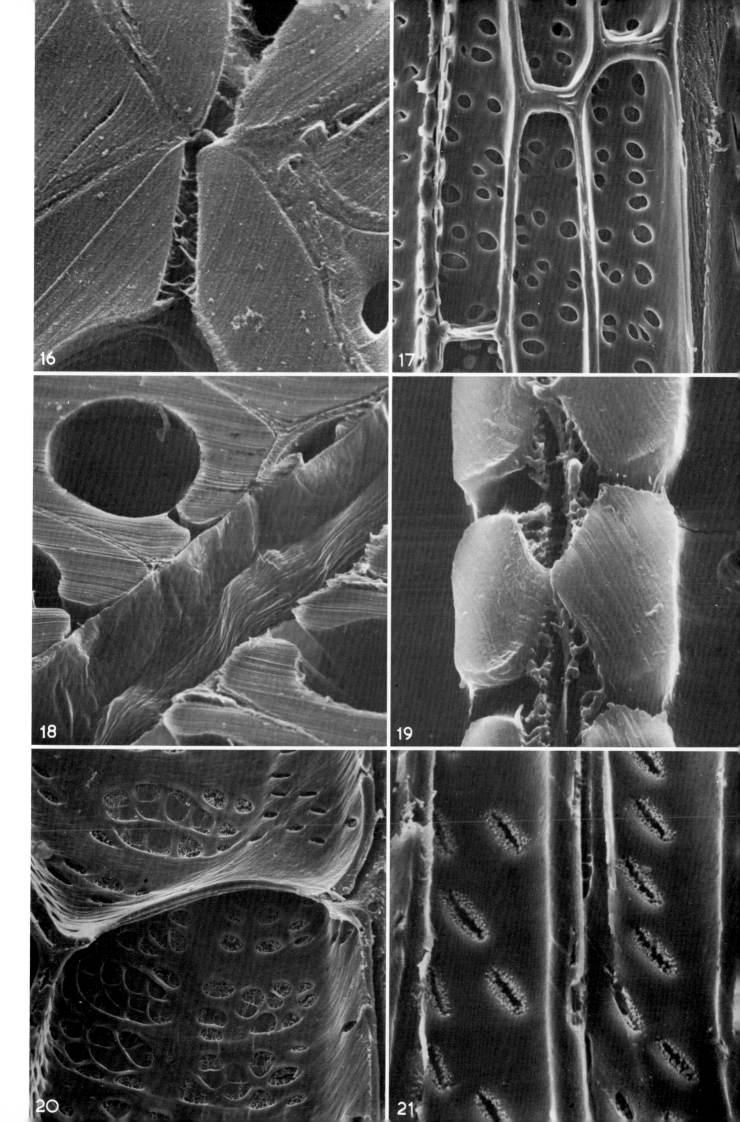

classify vestures on their morphology, no scheme so far proposed is entirely acceptable due to the large number of intermediate forms. In some woods, for example, the filamentous type can occur in the larger vessel to parenchyma pits but grade into small bead-like vestures in the smaller intervessel pits in the same cell.

The function of vestures in bordered pits is not clear though it has been suggested that they play a role in decreasing the risk of pit membrane rupture, caused by pressure drops between vessel elements arising from local air embolism [184]. Vestures may also occur on helical thickenings [103, 104] (Fig. 36) and perforation plate borders [22, 84] (Figs. 156 and 157) where there is no question of membrane involvement. It is worth noting that vestures may disappear in partly decomposed or fossil woods, making their value as a diagnostic feature of doubtful value in some cases.

1.3 Wall sculpturing

Helical or spiral thickenings in the secondary xylem are ridges of cell wall material, superimposed on a portion or the entire lumen surface of certain cells. The helix is defined as being either S or Z when the direction (as if viewed from the outside of the cell) is the same as the centre stroke of the letters S or Z. Helical thickenings usually make an S-helix [102, 103, 131] but may occasionally wind in a Z-direction [118, 131]. In most cases the orientation of the helical thickenings has the same general direction as the microfibrils of the S_3 layer of the secondary wall. Helical thickenings are known to occur as a regular feature in the axial tracheids of normal wood in several softwoods (Figs. 75, 76 and 78). They also occur in the compression wood tracheids of certain softwoods [160] (*see* Section 2.8). They are also a feature of the cell walls in the vessel elements [103, 118], fibres and vascular tracheids of many hardwoods, and have occasionally been observed in ray and axial parenchyma cells [173] (Fig. 187). Helical thickenings tend to be more frequent in the woody species of subtropical and temperate distribution [1, 27, 164] than in those of tropical distribution.

The thickenings are composed of aggregates of parallel bundles of microfibrils and are normally deposited on the S_3 wall layer [66]. The strength of their attachment to this layer varies considerably both between and within species. Some wood scientists have contended that helical thickenings are very loosely attached to the inside layer of the normal secondary wall [54, 77, 167, 169] and are overlaid at a slightly different angle to the orientation of the microfibrils in it, others have suggested that helical thickenings are an integral part of the secondary wall [30, 176]. Still others have regarded them as homologous with the other layers of the secondary wall and suggested that they could represent an attempt to

Fig. 22. Vestures in intervessel pits and spread out over the lumen surface in *Leptospermum ericoides* A. Rich. (Myrtaceae) showing the close morphological relationship between vestures and particles of the warty layer. RLF × 6800.

Fig. 23. Vestured intervessel pits in *Leptospermum scoparium* J. R. et G. Forst. (Myrtaceae). Note the fine particles of the warty layer adhering to the S_3 layer. RLF × 8000.

Fig. 24. Vestured intervessel pits in *Carmichaelia angustata* Kirk (Leguminaceae). On the right hand side of this micrograph the wall of the vessel nearest the reader has been removed revealing the pit chambers. TLF × 7300.

Fig. 25. Vestures lining the chamber wall of a vessel bordered pit in *Leptospermum scoparium* exposed by removing the adjacent cell and the pit membrane TLF × 19000.

Fig. 26. Vestured intervessel pits in *Persoonia toru* A. Gunn. (Proteaceae). In this wood the vestures protrude from the inner pit apertures and completely obscure the pits, often spreading beyond them on the lumen surface of the vessel wall. RLF × 6500.

Fig. 27. Vestures spreading out onto the lumen surface of a fibre wall in *Persoonia toru*. RLF × 3500.

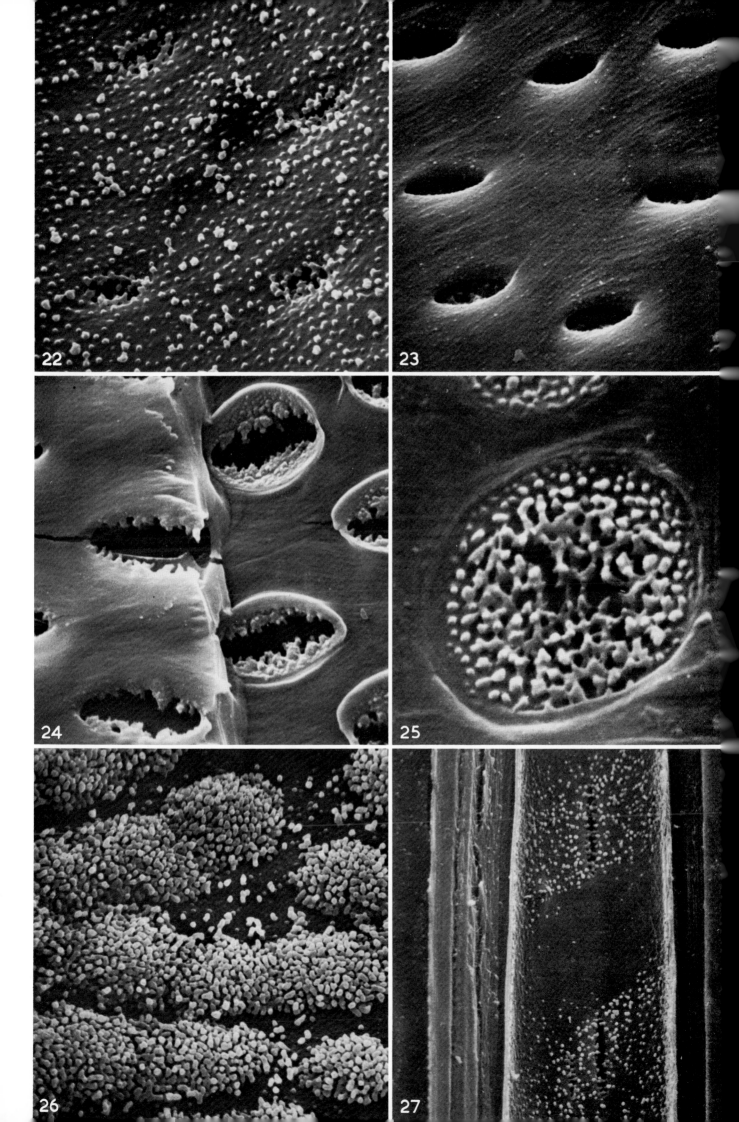

continue secondary wall formation at a time when the life of the cell is drawing to its close.

The thickenings may form a single helix or a series of parallel helices winding around the cell lumen. They may be branched or unbranched. Some woods are characterized by the presence of one type of thickening only, while in other woods several different types of thickening may be found. Several attempts have been made to classify helical thickenings. One scheme separated them into (i) unbranched; (ii) branched, and (iii) swirled [131]. A second scheme is based on the dominant winding angle, separating helices into (i) predominantly S helix; (ii) predominantly Z helix; (iii) S and Z helices; further subdividing each class into unbranched and branched [118]. A third scheme is based on the prominence of the thickenings [103]. Under this scheme four types of helical thickenings can be recognized. These are designated: (i) fine striations; (ii) light helical thickenings sometimes merging with the vessel wall; (iii) prominent helical thickenings and (iv) very close prominent helical thickenings. Fine striations appear as fine checks or grooves in the S_3 wall layer (Fig. 28). Light helical thickenings are defined as ridges of wall material clearly overlying the vessel S_3 wall but not standing out from it (Fig. 29). Such thickenings often merge with the vessel wall. Prominent helical thickenings are defined as ridges of wall material commonly standing out from the normal S_3 wall layer (Fig. 30), while very close prominent helical thickenings are defined as deep ridges, very close together, and covering the entire cell wall (Fig. 31).

Woods whose vessels have prominent or very close prominent helical thickenings are more likely to have such thickenings present in all the vessels than those woods that have only faint striations or light helical thickenings. When helical thickenings are only sporadically present or poorly developed in a species they may be confined to one part of the cell only. Some authorities state that the thickenings in tracheids and fibres are usually more obvious near the middle of the cells [142, 167], while others note that some cells, such as the vessels in *Liquidamber* and *Nyssa* show spirals only in the cell ends [122].

The pitch of the helical thickenings varies little with cell diameter (Figs. 32 and 33) and the claim that narrow lumened cells have steeper pitched thickenings than wider lumened cells [122] may be the exception rather than the rule [103]. Marked differences in the helical winding angle between adjacent cells do occur occasionally but bear little relationship to the cell diameter (Fig. 34). Smaller diameter cells have larger and more prominent thickenings than larger ones [118]. In *Robinia pseudoacacia* L. and *Ulmus procera* Salisb., for example, the small vessels have steep prominent helical thickenings while the larger vessels are devoid of thickenings.

Fig. 28. Fine striations on the walls of vessel elements in *Beilschmiedia tawa* (A. Cunn.) Benth. et Hook.f. (Lauraceae). RLF × 750.

Fig. 29. Light helical thickenings, sometimes merging with the vessel wall, in *Carpodetus serratus* J. R. et G. Forst. (Escalloniaceae). RLF × 1500.

Fig. 30. Prominent helical thickenings standing out from the normal S_3 layer in *Hoheria angustifolia* Raoul. (Malvaceae). RLF × 800.

Fig. 31. Very close prominent helical thickenings covering the entire vessel wall in *Myrsine australia* (A. Rich.) Allan. (Myrsinaceae). RLF × 2500.

Fig. 32. Helical thickenings on the vessel walls of *Cassinia fulvida* Hook.f. (Compositae). Although the pit apertures indicate a marked difference in the angle of the microfibrils of the S_2 layer between the narrow central cell and the wider outer cells, the helical winding angle of the helical thickenings remains constant. RLF × 2300.

Fig. 33. Helical thickenings showing a similar helical winding angle despite marked differences in the tracheid diameter in *Pseudotsuga menziesii* Franco. (Pinaceae). RLF × 700.

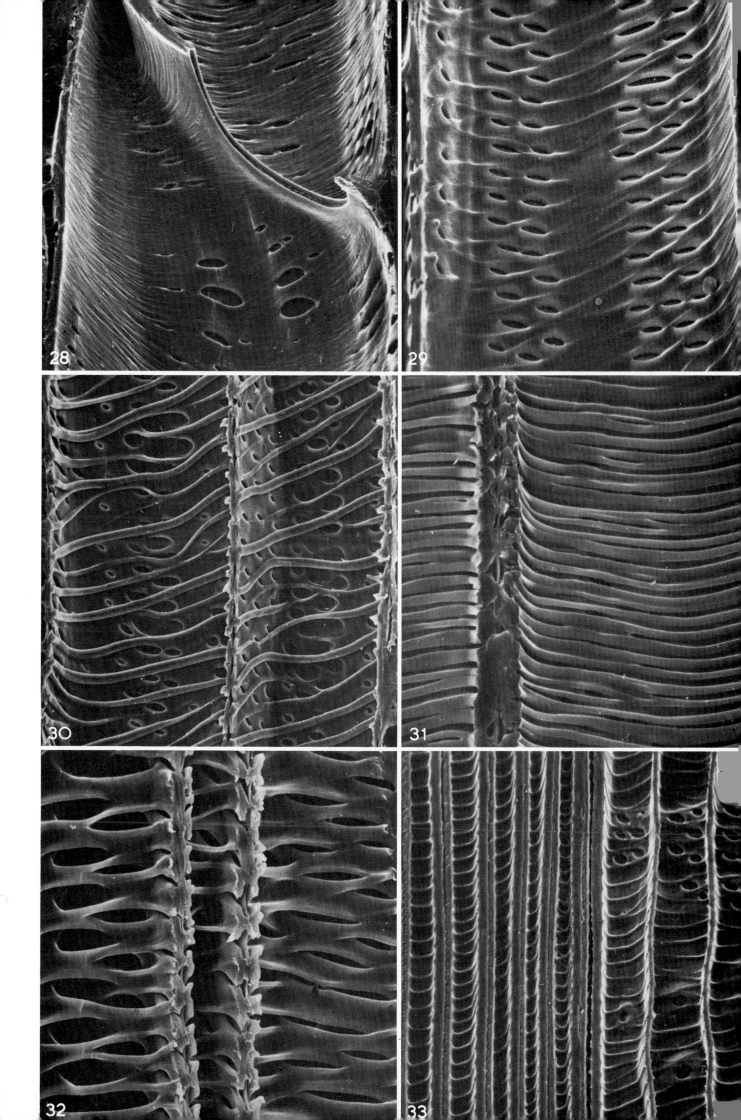

Although the helical thickenings usually wind in an S-direction, this orientation is often obscured near perforation plates where changes in the helical winding angle often occur and complicated swirling patterns may result (Fig. 36). The normal pattern is also modified near pits, the thickenings deviating in order to pass between the pit apertures, though bridging of the pit apertures can occur [103] (Fig. 37).

Two other types of wall sculpturing termed *callitrisoid* thickenings and *crassulae* are confined to softwoods and these are described in Section 2.3.

1.4 Trabeculae

Trabeculae are extensions of cell wall material that occasionally traverse the lumina of wood cells. They are well known in softwoods where they can be seen in the transverse or radial longitudinal face traversing several tracheids in a radial row [81] (Fig. 38). They can also occur in hardwoods where they may traverse many different cell types in a radial file including vessel elements, axial parenchyma cells and fibres [26] (Fig. 41). Most trabeculae are thin and rod shaped, but shorter, thicker, spool shaped varieties have also been observed as well as ones of irregular form [112]. While trabeculae are commonly seen traversing several cells in a radial file, solitary trabeculae traversing the lumina of single cells, although much more difficult to recognize at low magnification, are possibly more common in both softwoods and hardwoods (Figs. 39 and 92).

Trabeculae normally have a central core surrounded by a thick layer of cell wall material [18] (Fig. 40). The nature of the core has not been determined, but it appears to have structural continuity with the middle lamella. It is affected in the same way by delignifying agents and a wide variety of histochemical stains. The central core is continuous with the intercellular layer of the tangential walls of the tracheid or vessel element [112] and is sometimes visible when the trabecula is pitted [98]. The zone enclosing the core has a structural continuity with the secondary wall of the cell. Polarized light microscopy and the presence of slip planes or compression dislocations in the trabecula indicates that the orientation of the cellulose microfibrils is parallel to the long axis of the trabecula [81, 112]. The similarity in appearance of softwood and hardwood trabeculae suggests that the causal mechanism responsible for their development is probably the same in both groups of plants.

At least two theories have been proposed to explain the origin of trabeculae. One theory suggests that their development starts in the vascular cambium when a cell wall is deposited over a thin fungal hypha [59]. In some way this structure is then perpetuated in further cells derived from the same cambial initial giving rise to the

Fig. 34. Wide differences in the helical winding angle between adjacent cells is unusual. Such a difference is seen here between two vessel elements in *Pseudopanax edgerleyi* (Hook.f.) C. Koch (Araliaceae). RLF × 625.

Fig. 35. An unusual form of helical thickenings on the vessel walls of *Clematis paniculata* Gmel. (Ranunculaceae). RLF × 1350.

Fig. 36. Prominent helical thickenings 'swirling' near the end of a vessel element in *Sophora microphylla* Ait. (Papilionaceae). Note the vestures adhering to the helical thickenings. RLF × 1150.

Fig. 37. Light helical thickenings on a vessel wall in *Nestegis cunninghamii* (Hook.f.) L. Johnson (Oleaceae). Note the helical thickenings apparently crossing four pit apertures (arrowed). RLF × 2700.

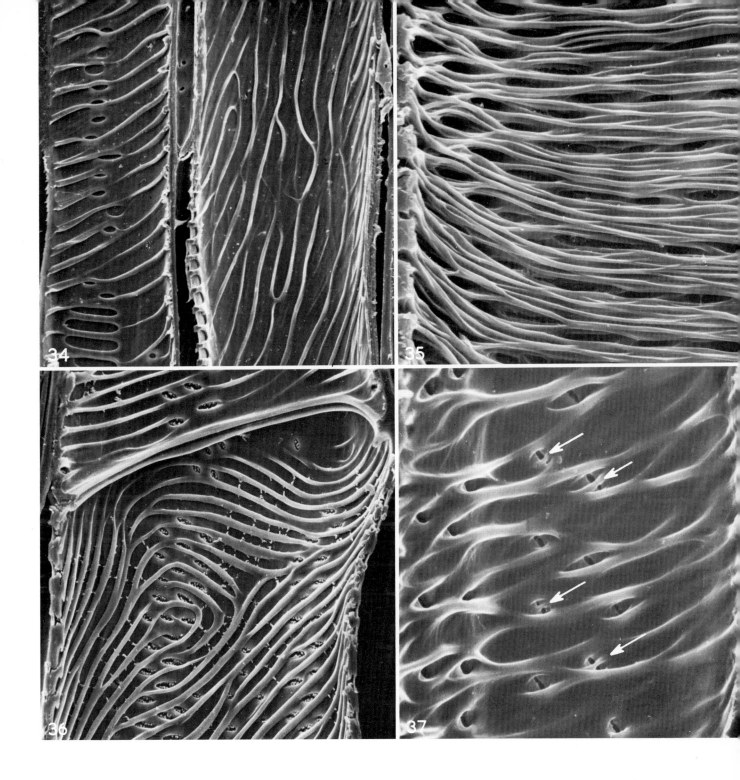

typical radial file of trabeculae. It has been claimed that the theory of fungal origin is further supported by the fact that trabeculae occur more frequently in regions where the cambium has been exposed to infection [60]. They are also supposed to be more frequently associated with other abnormalities known to be caused by fungi. Certainly trabeculae can extend across several annual growth layers so the causal mechanism, whatever it might be, must be able to restart after a period of dormancy. A second theory suggests that trabeculae are initiated by the effects of low temperatures in the active cambium, probably by the influence of late and early frosts in spring or late summer [105]. Neither of these possible causal factors have been verified and it is likely that other explanations are possible. A periclinal division, for example, in either the fusiform initial or the xylem mother cells such that the cell plate fused with a side wall at some point could produce a rod in one daughter cell when radial expansion of the cells followed. Repeated periclinal division in a xylem mother cell with such a rod would then perpetuate this abnormality in a number of cells in a radial file.

In hardwoods, the diameter of the trabecula is related to the lumen diameter and cell wall thickness of the host cell [26, 112]. A trabecula traversing several different cell types in a radial file tends to be thin and cylindrical in cells with thin walls and large lumina, and to be thick and spool shaped in cells with thick walls and narrow lumina (Fig. 41). This feature adds further weight to the theory that trabeculae develop by the deposition of the normal secondary wall around a filament. In addition to the changes that occur as the trabecula passes from one cell type to another in a file, a gradual transition from rod-like to spool-shaped sometimes occurs towards the end of a long trabecula.

1.5 Cell inclusions

The lumina of living and dead wood cells of both softwoods and hardwoods sometimes contain a variety of substances variously described as *cell inclusions* or *extraneous* materials. These may take the form of crystals, grains or plates, or simply an amorphous mass inside the cell. The main inorganic inclusions are calcium crystals and silica grains, while the organic substances include gums, resins, tannins, oils and starch.

1.5.1 *Crystals*

Crystals, although found in a few softwoods, are more common in hardwoods, particularly those of tropical origin. The most common consist of variously shaped deposits of calcium oxalate [111, 149], though crystals of calcium carbonate [35, 149] and more rarely calcium phosphate have been recorded.

Crystals are usually formed in the axial and ray

Fig. 38. Part of a trabecula traversing several tracheids (T) and an axial parenchyma cell (AP) in a radial file in *Sequoia sempervirens* Endl. (Taxodiaceae). RLF × 1100.

Fig. 39. A trabecula traversing only one tracheid in *Cryptomeria japonica* (L.f.) D. Don (Taxodiaceae). Note the fine warty layer and the pit aperture RLF × 2200.

Fig. 40. Cross section through a trabecula in *Knightia excelsa* R.Br. (Proteaceae). The trabecula shows a three layered structure consisting of a central core surrounded by a thicker layer of wall material comparable in thickness to the S_2 layer, which is in turn ensheathed by a thin outer layer. TLF × 11 000.

Fig. 41. Part of a trabecula traversing a vessel element, (V) an axial parenchyma cell (P) and several fibres (F) in a radial file in *Coprosma repens*. A. Rich. (Rubiaceae). The diameter of the trabecula is generally proportional to thickness of the wall of the cell through which it is passing. (The breaks occurred during specimen examination). TF × 1450.

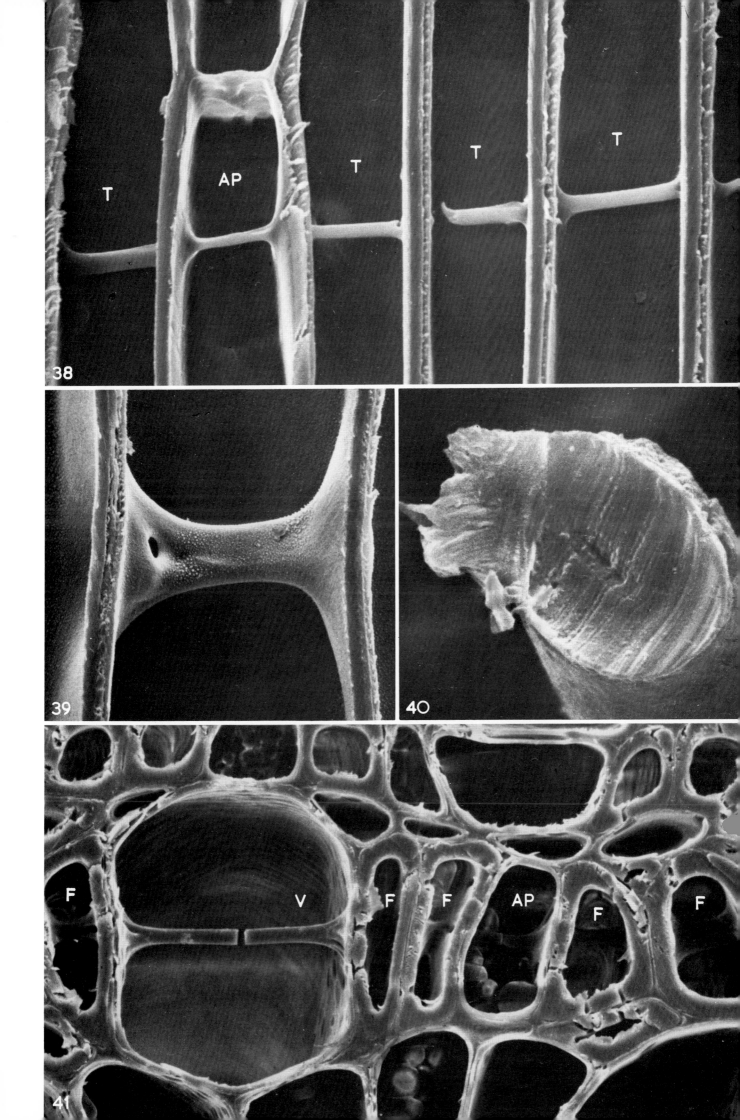

parenchyma cells, though they may also occur in septate fibres, tyloses and more rarely in vessels. In vessels their presence is usualy associated with fungal contamination (Fig. 42). In axial parenchyma, crystals may occupy one or all of the cells in the strand. Occasionally the axial parenchyma cells which bear crystals are chambered (Figs. 43 and 188) by the development of fine unlignified cross walls by a division process similar to that which produces septate fibres (*see* Section 4.5). In the rays, crystals tend to be more common in the upright cells particularly at the vertical extremities [122].

The larger calcium oxalate crystals tend to develop either as *rhomboidal* structures occupying almost the entire cell (Fig. 45) or as bundles of small parallel crystals termed *raphides* (Figs. 44 and 46). (Raphides are also commonly found in woody monocotyledons (Figs. 123 – 125) . Masses of fine minute crystals of granular appearance are referred to as *crystal sand*. Crystals develop within the vacuoles of the living cell and it is not uncommon to find them still enclosed in a membrane or sac long after the cell cytoplasm has died (Fig. 47). These sacs, which may show fine 'pits' in their walls (Fig. 48) are unaffected by hydrochloric acid but are readily removed by sodium hydroxide [65].

The presence or absence of crystals is of very limited value as a taxonomic character in wood identification.

1.5.2 *Silica grains*

Deposits of silica as grains or granulated lumps are a feature of the axial and ray parenchyma cells [64, 148, 172, 174] and septate fibres of certain woods, particularly tropical hardwoods [12, 65]. Silica inclusions have irregular surfaces (Fig. 50) and are sometimes responsible for the rapid blunting of cutting tools. Silica may also form a wall lining on the lumen surface of vessel elements [64] and some other axial wood cells.

1.5.3 *Starch*

Starch grains are common in axial and ray parenchyma cells of the sapwood of both softwoods (Figs. 88 and 89) and hardwoods (Fig. 49) and also occur in hardwood fibres (Fig. 173). They are frequently spherical in shape.

1.5.4 *Resins and gums*

Dark coloured organic substances, known as *resins* in softwoods and *gums* in hardwoods, occur in some woods. Their chemical composition varies considerably from one wood to another. Resin may occur between the axial or ray elements in specialized *ducts* or *canals* (Fig. 52) or form within the cells as *plates* or *wall linings* (*see* Section 2.7). Similarly gums may be deposited in vessel elements (Fig. 51), fibres and parenchyma cells or form in intercellular canals or ducts (*see* Section 4.8). Both resins and gums can develop in response to injury and may be found in the large lens shaped pockets known as shakes.

Fig. 42. Small crystals adhering to a vessel wall in *Melicytus micranthus* Hook.f. (Violaceae). They are often associated with fungal contamination. RLF × 2700.

Fig. 43. Crystals in chambered parenchyma cells in *Cyathodes fasciculata* (Forst.f.) Allan (Epacridacae). RLF × 2000.

Fig. 44. Raphide crystals in an axial parenchyma cell of *Coprosma areolata* Cheesem. (Rubiaceae) RLF × 600.

Fig. 45. Rhomboidal crystals in the ray cells of *Pseudopanax discolor* (Kirk) Harms (Araliaceae). Note starch grains in right hand cell (arrowed). TLF × 2100.

Fig. 46. Raphides in a thin walled parenchyma cell of *Heimleriodendron brunonianum* (Endl.) Skottsb. (Nyctaginaceae). These crystals have all been cut in one plane during specimen preparation. TF × 1200.

Fig. 47. Crystals enclosed in a membrane or sac (arrowed) in the ray cells of *Griselinia lucida* Forst.f. (Griseliniaceae). The roughened surfaces of these crystals are due to cutting during specimen preparation. RLF × 525.

Fig. 48. Crystal sac in a ray cell of *Melicytus ramiflorus* J. R. et G. Forst. (Violaceae). Note the pit-like areas on the sac. TLF × 2200.

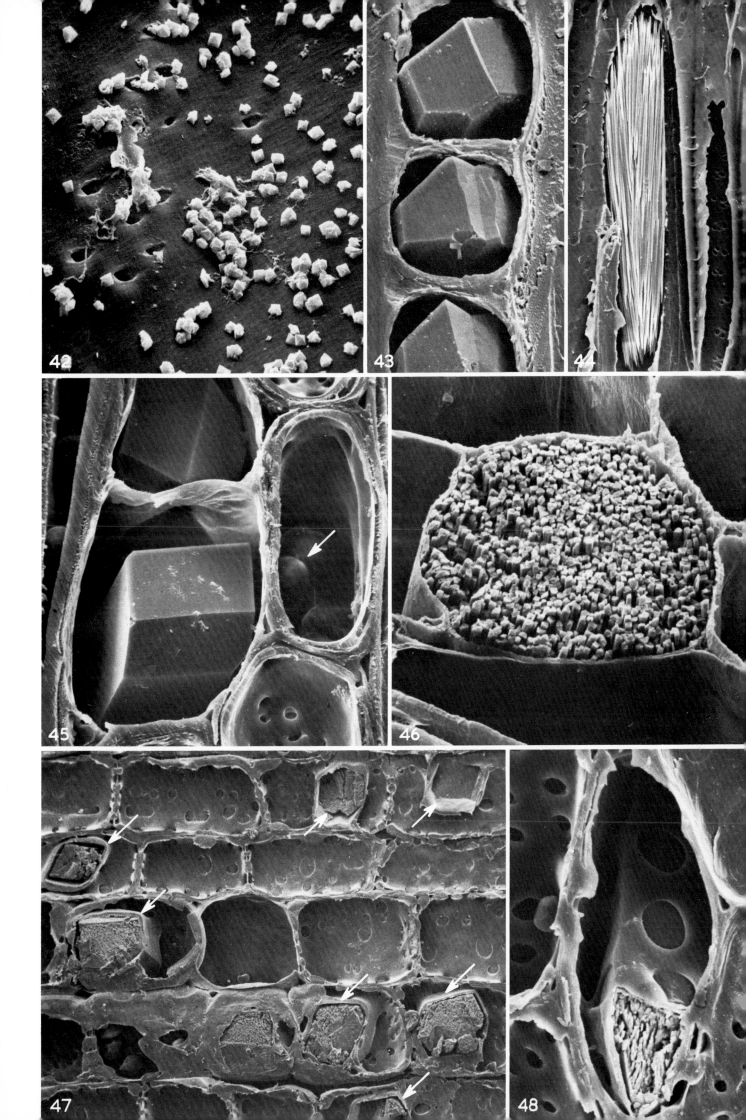

Vessels in some woods have occasionally been observed plugged with a mixture of polyphenolic substances and calcium salts [153]. This effect is possibly associated with tylosis [76].

1.5.5 *Other extraneous materials*

Oils, tannins, alkaloids, fats and fatty acids, sugars and latex are among the list of other complex organic materials often found in wood. Their chemistry and distribution, however, lie outside the scope of this volume.

Fig. 49. Starch grains in an axial parenchyma cell of *Myoporum laetum* Forst.f. (Myoporaceae). TLF × 4500.

Fig. 50. A granulated silica lump in a septate fibre of *Dysoxylum spectabile* (Forst.f.) Hook.f. (Meliaceae). RLF × 6500.

Fig. 51. A gummy deposit in a vessel of *Pseudopanax aboreus* (Murr.) Philipson (Araliaceae). TLF × 1800.

Fig. 52. Resin in the epithelial parenchyma cells of an axial resin canal in *Pinus radiata* D.Don (Pinaceae). RLF × 475.

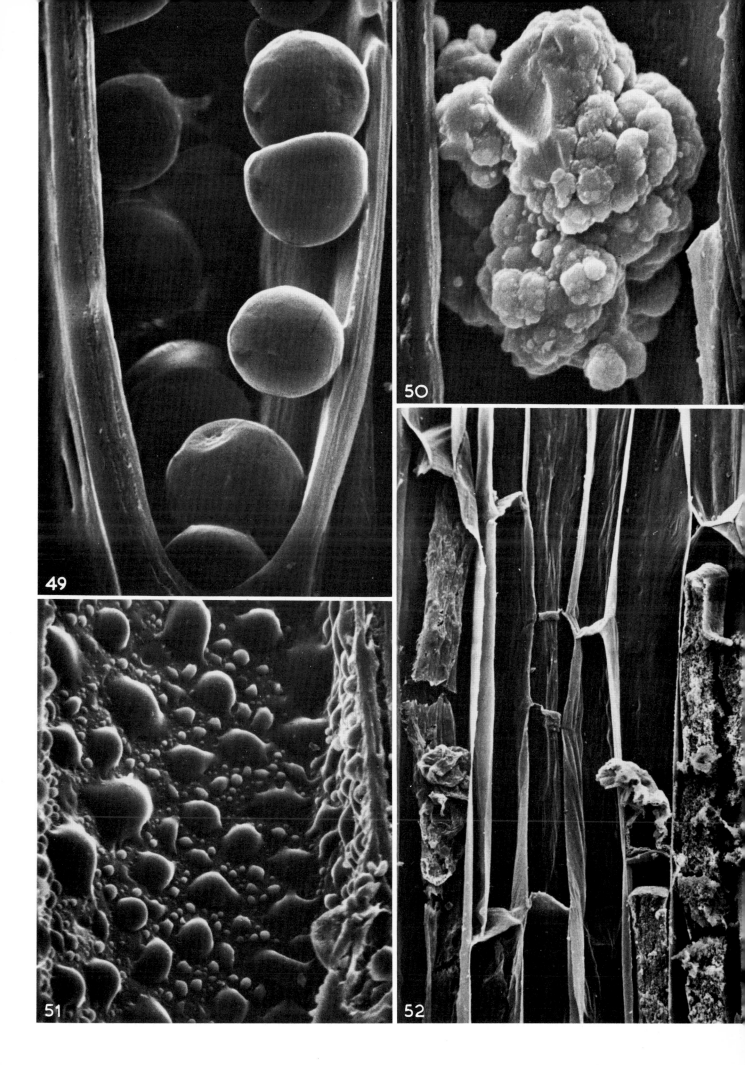

2   The Structure of softwoods

The secondary xylem of the conifers is commonly called *softwood*. This term can at times be misleading, however, as many coniferous woods are physically quite hard while some angiosperm *hardwoods* are, in fact, quite soft (e.g. balsa). Softwoods are simpler and more homogeneous in structure than hardwoods. The greater bulk of the axial cell system is made up of tracheids which function both in water conduction and support (Figs. 53 and 54). Some softwoods also have axial parenchyma cells but these are never as abundant as in hardwoods. Fibres and vessel elements are absent. Resin excreting epithelial cells and strand tracheids are the only other axial elements present, and these occur in a few softwoods only. The ray system is built up mostly of thin walled parenchyma cells with ray tracheids and horizontal resin canals present in some woods.

Despite the apparent simplicity of conifer wood, it appears to function very efficiently when one considers the height attained by the trunks of some trees such as the giant North American redwoods *Sequoia sempervirens* D. Don. and the weight of foliage borne by such stems.

2.1 Growth increments

The cyclic pattern of seasonal cambial activity in most softwoods produces a series of growth rings that are visible in the transverse and radial longitudinal faces of a cut stem (Fig. 55). In some softwoods the growth ring boundary between the latewood tracheids of one growth ring and the earlywood tracheids of the next ring is very sharp and the ring boundary is classified as *very distinct* or *distinct* (Figs. 33, 55 and 56). In other woods, or even the same wood produced under less severe climatic conditions, the latewood to earlywood transition can be less dramatic and the boundary is described as *moderately* or *slightly distinct* (Fig. 58). Growth ring boundaries that cannot be detected except by microscopy are usually described as *indistinct* (Fig. 57). Growth ring boundaries may be smooth and regular or wavy and irregular in outline (Fig. 58).

Earlywood is characterized by having large lumened, thin-walled tracheids each having a large number of intertracheid pits of the conifer raised border type (*see* section 1.2). Except in the first few rows of earlywood tracheids and last few rows of latewood tracheids in each growth ring, these pits are usually confined to the radial walls (Fig. 59) where they are most frequent near the cell tips. Latewood is characterized by having longer, smaller lumened, thicker-walled tracheids with fewer pits than earlywood. These pits are of the reduced bordered pit

Fig. 53. Transverse and trangential longitudinal faces of the softwood *Pinus nigra* Schneid. (Pinaceae). The wood is built up of axial tracheids (T), with ray parenchyma and ray tracheids grouped into predominantly uniseriate rays (R). Axial parenchyma is absent. Resin canals can be seen in the transverse face (RC) and also in a multiseriate ray (RC). TF/TLF × 175.

Fig. 54. Transverse and tangential longitudinal faces of the softwood *Podocarpus dacrydioides* A. Rich. (Podocarpaceae). The wood is built up of axial tracheids and thin walled axial parenchyma cells, and parenchymatous uniseriate rays. Resin canals and ray tracheids are absent. TF/TLF × 300.

Fig. 55. A growth ring boundary in *Chamaecyparis lawsoniana* Parl. (Cupressaceae). Note the thicker walled, smaller lumened tracheids in the latewood and the thinner walled larger lumened tracheids in the earlywood. Conifer bordered pits are prolific on the radial walls of the tracheids throughout the growth rings. TF/RLF × 400.

Fig. 56. A distinct growth ring boundary in *Pseudotsuga menziesii* Franco (Pinaceae). TF × 110.

Fig. 57. An indistinct growth ring boundary in *Dacrydium cupressinum* Lamb. (Podocarpaceae). TF × 80.

Fig. 58. A moderately distinct growth ring with a wavy outline in *Dacrydium biforme* (Hook.) Pilger (Podocarpaceae). TF × 175.

Fig. 59. Intertracheid bordered pits are confined to the radial walls in most softwoods except the last few tracheids in the latewood and the first few tracheids in the early wood of each growth ring. In these tracheids they also occur frequently on the tangential wall as seen in this radial longitudinal face of *Cedrus libani* (Pinaceae). RLF × 550.

Fig. 60. Transverse view of a growth ring boundary in *Agathis australis* Salisb. (Araucariaceae). Note that a single ray cell traverses the latewood – earlywood boundary. This suggests that several new tracheids were produced by the cambial fusiform cells before the ray cambial cell divided periclinally. TF × 700.

Figs. 55 to 60 are on page 30.

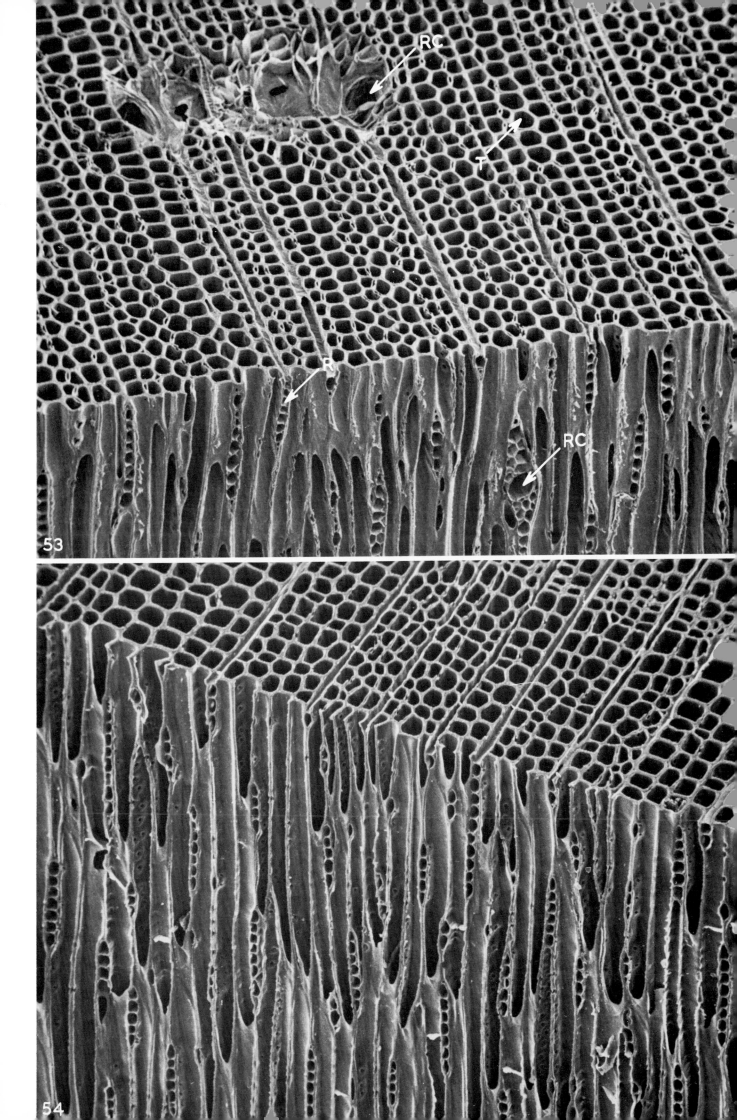

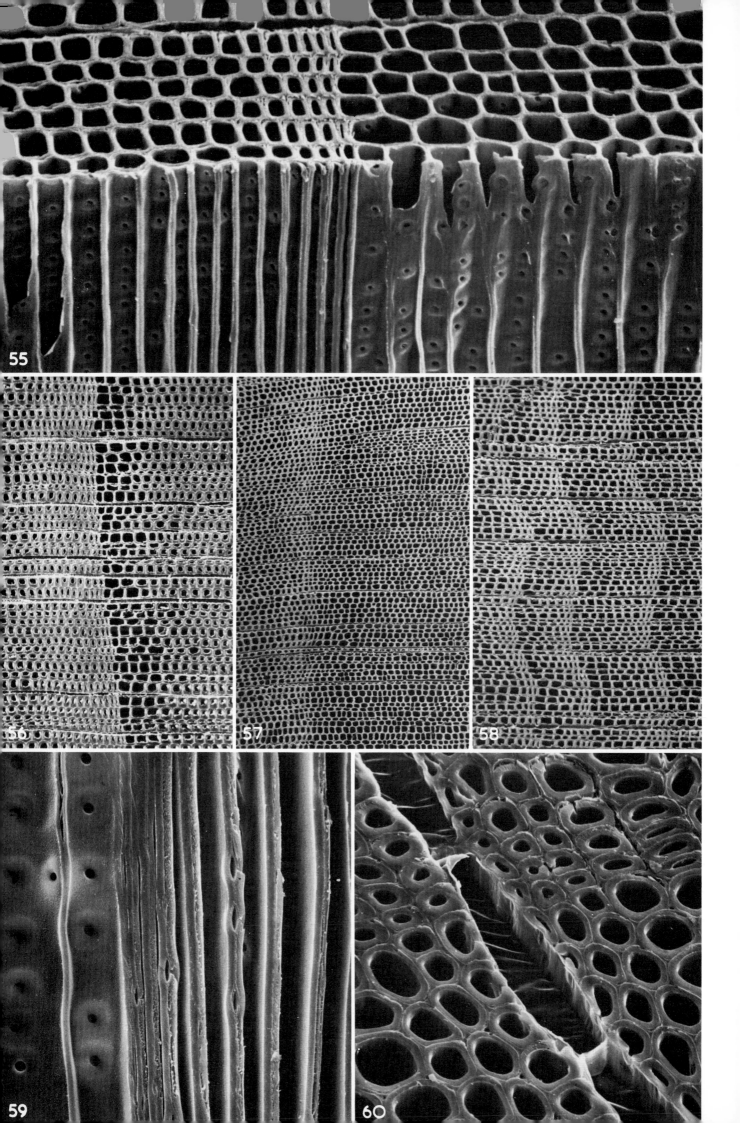

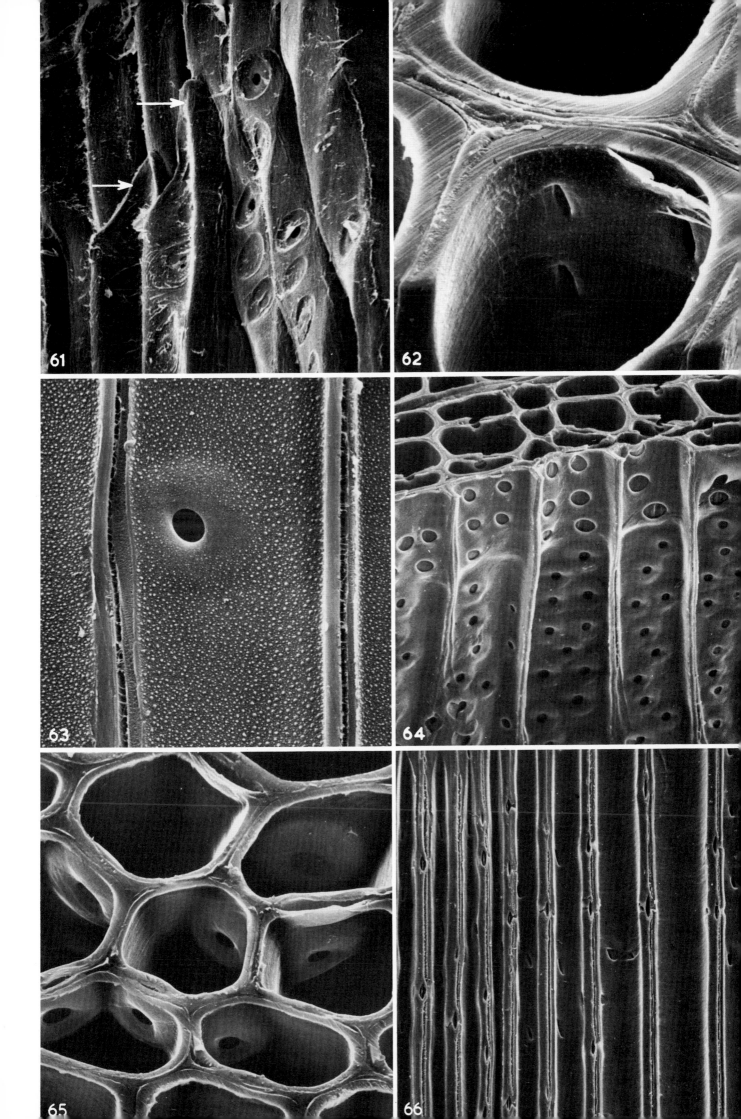

Fig. 61. Tracheids exposed by separating the cells in partly macerated wood of *Pinus radiata* D.Don (Pinaceae). The narrow cell tips (arrowed) indicate the approximate extent of the intrusive growth of the tracheids. RLF fractured wall. × 900

Fig. 62. Structure of the tracheid wall in *Pinus radiata* latewood. Three zones can be distinguished: the middle lamella, primary walls and secondary S_1 layer: overlaid by the thick S_2 layer which is in turn overlaid by the thinner S_3 layer (separated slightly to the right of the micrograph). TF/RLF × 2600.

Fig. 63. A warty layer lining the lumen surface of the secondary wall in tracheids of *Cedrus libani* RLF × 1650.

Fig. 64. Large cupressoid tracheid to ray simple (top) and intertracheid bordered (bottom) pits interrupting the secondary walls of tracheids in *Podocarpus dacrydioides* A. Rich. (Podocarpaceae). TF/RLF × 700.

Fig. 65. Intertracheid conifer bordered pits in *Pinus nigra* Schneid. (Pinaceae). TF × 1450.

Fig. 66. Intertracheid pits on the tangential as well as the radial walls in *Phyllocladus trichomanoides* Don. (Podocarpaceae). RLF × 500

Figs. 61 to 66 are on page 31.

Fig. 67. Uniseriate intertracheid conifer bordered pitting in *Cupressus arizonica* Greene (Cupressaceae). RLF × 1150.

Fig. 68. Biseriate intertracheid conifer bordered pitting arranged predominantly in an opposite manner in *Taxodium distichum* Rich. (Taxodiaceae). RLF × 1150.

Fig. 69. Multiseriate intertracheid conifer bordered pitting arranged in an alternate manner in *Araucaria cunninghamii* Sweet (Araucariaceae). RLF × 550.

Fig. 70. A uniseriate ray in *Pinus nigra* Schnied. (Pinaceae) built up of ray tracheids (RT) (upper and lower extremities), thin-walled ray parenchyma cells (P) and intercellular spaces (IS). Note the different pit types connecting the axial tracheid to the ray tracheids (arrowed) and to the ray parenchyma. TLF × 2300.

Fig. 71. Tracheid to ray cross field pitting in *Araucaria cunninghamii*. These tracheid to ray pits are of the cupressoid type. RLF × 600.

Fig. 72. Window-like tracheid to ray cross field pitting in *Dacrydium colensoi* Hook. (Podocarpaceae). RLF × 1250.

Fig. 73. Cupressoid tracheid to ray cross field pitting in *Cupressus fortulosa* D. Don. (Cupressaceae). RLF × 600.

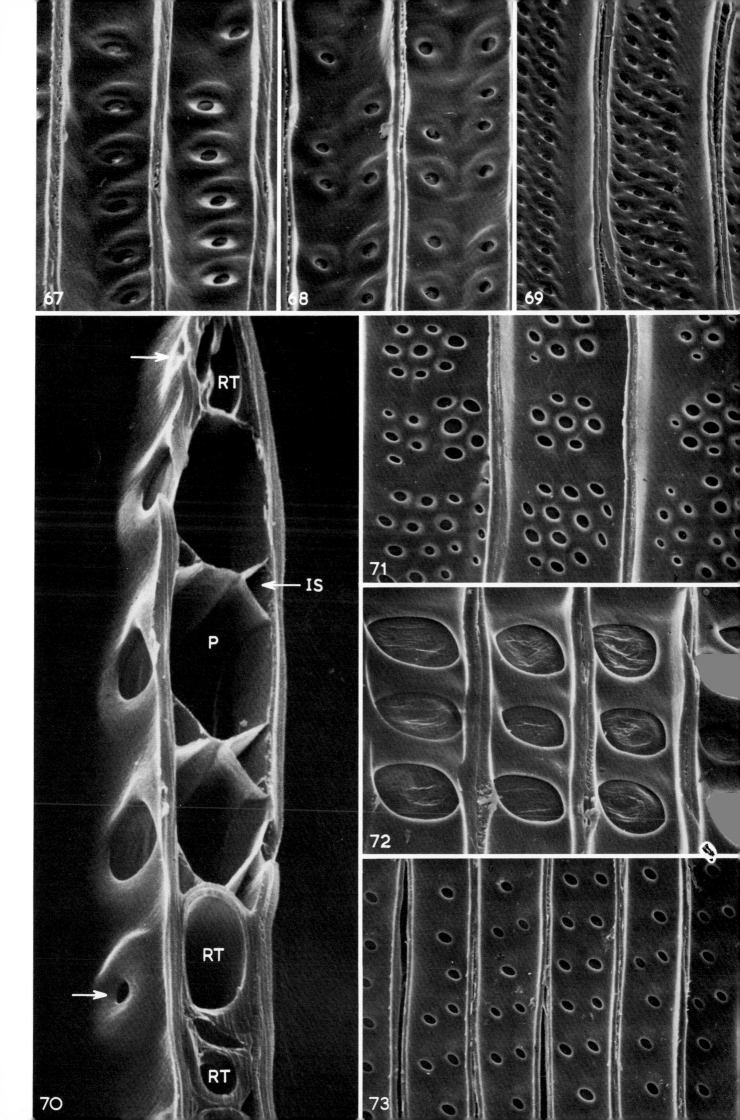

67

68

69

RT

IS

P

RT

RT

70

71

72

73

type and occur on the tangential as well as the radial walls in some woods. These changes are in keeping with the transition in function from primarily conduction to primarily support that accompanies the gradation from earlywood to latewood across a growth ring.

Rays passing from near the stem centre outwards to the vascular cambium normally traverse many growth increments. The individual ray parenchyma cells are usually longer in radial extent in the earlywood than in the latewood. Ray cells do not always possess a tangential end wall at the ring boundary, and individual ray cells may extend from the latewood, well into the earlywood (Fig. 60). This phenomenon suggests that the fusiform initials divide periclinally several times (resulting in the development of several new tracheids) before the ray initials divide to cut off a new ray cell.

2.2 Tracheids and tracheid pitting

In the conifers, the functions of both axial conduction and support are performed by the one cell type – the *tracheid* (Figs. 53 and 54). Tracheids are axially elongated cells with pointed ends and have no living contents at functional maturity. Although they may attain lengths of up to 10 mm in some woods, they are usually of the order of 1 to 5 mm long depending on the tree species, the radial distance from the stem centre, the position in the growth increment and the height in the tree. The cell tips, which are more sharply pointed in the tangential than radial plane, are densely intertwined (Fig. 61). This cell arrangement results from the non-storeyed nature of the fusiform cambial initials in the vascular cambium of coniferous species and helps to give the wood its high 'along the grain' strength. The radial dimensions of the tracheids vary depending on the position in the growth increment but are usually of the order of 0.01 to 0.08 mm.

Tracheids possess secondarily thickened cell walls (*see* Section 1.1). Except in the modified tracheids found in the underside of leaning stems, the wall structure consists of a $P + S_1 + S_2 + S_3$ arrangement with the S_2 layer making up 50 per cent or more of the total wall thickness (Fig. 62). The cellulose microfibrils of the S_2 layer are generally orientated at a steep angle to the long axis of the cell and are enveloped between the $P + S_1$ and S_3 layers, a structure which gives the tracheid its remarkable strength properties. A warty layer may line the lumen surface of the tracheid secondary wall in some species [3, 4, 155] (Figs. 63 and 78).

Tracheid walls are pierced by a large number of pits. These may pair with pits in the neighbouring tracheids (Figs. 62, 63 and 65), axial parenchyma cells (Fig. 91), ray parenchyma cells (Figs. 64, 71 – 73) or ray tracheids (Fig. 70).

Pits leading to adjacent tracheids are termed

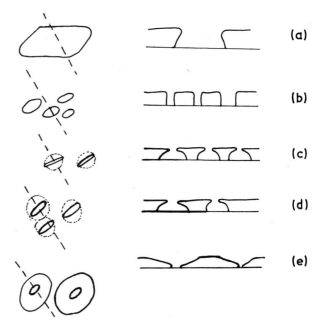

Fig. 74. Diagrammatic representation of the five main types of tracheid to ray pitting: (a) Fenestriform or window-like, (b) Pinoid, (c) Piceoid, (d) Cupressoid, (e) Taxodioid.

Fig. 75. Helical thickenings lining the tracheid walls in *Pseudotsuga menziesii* Franco (Pinaceae). TF/RLF × 850.

Fig. 76. Helical thickenings lining the tracheid walls in *Taxus baccata* L. (Taxaceae). TF/RLF × 1200.

Fig. 77. Wall splits in tracheids of *Podocarpus hallii* Kirk (Podocarpaceae). Such splits are a drying phenomenon and possibly indicate incipient compression wood. They can sometimes be mistaken for fine helical thickenings in light microscope wood preparations. RLF × 1550.

Fig. 78. Callitrisoid thickenings in a tracheid of *Callitris glauca* R.Br. (Cupressaceae). Note the entire wall surface is overlaid by a fine warty layer. RLF × 3000.

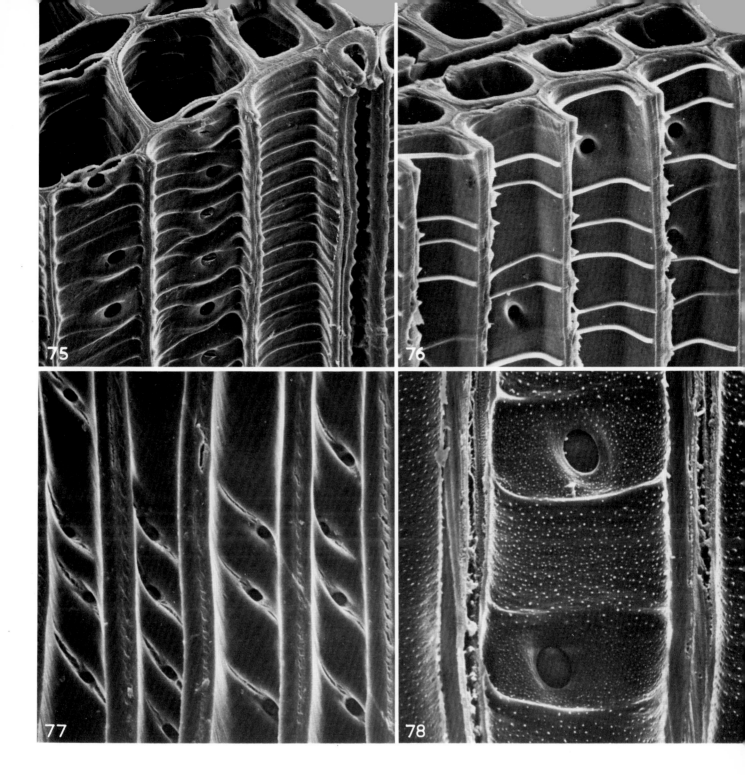

intertracheid pits. These occur predominantly on the radial walls. In some woods they are normally confined to the radial walls but in others they also occur on the tangential walls of the last few tracheids of the latewood and the first few tracheids of the earlywood. In a few species they are found on both radial and tangential walls of the tracheids throughout the growth ring (Fig. 66). Intertracheid pits may lie in one row per tracheid (uniseriate) (Fig. 67), two rows (biseriate) (Fig. 68), or several rows (multiseriate) (Fig. 69). Multiseriate intertracheid pitting is almost always *opposite* (Fig. 68), but *alternate* pitting can occur occasionally in a variety of woods and is the normal arrangement in *Agathis* and *Araucaria* (Fig. 69).

Pits connecting tracheids to axial parenchyma cells are often smaller than the intertracheid pits (Fig. 91). They do not usually have raised borders nor do the pit membranes have a centrally thickened torus. The pit apertures may be larger than the intertracheid pit apertures and are commonly elliptical.

Pits connecting tracheids to ray cells are grouped into prominent *cross fields* (Figs. 70 – 74). Although these pits generally have borders overarching simple pit membranes, the size and shape of the apertures in a species is generally sufficiently characteristic to enable this feature to be of considerable taxonomic significance.

Five types are recognized [75].

(a) *Fenestriform* or *window-like* pits (Figs. 72 and 74a) are large and almost simple. They occur in *Dacrydium*, *Phyllocladus* and certain other genera including a few pines.

(b) *Cupressoid* pits (Figs. 64, 73, 74b and 94) vary in size and have elliptical apertures bordered on the two long sides. They occur in *Cupressus*, *Taxus*, *Araucaria* and certain other genera.

(c) *Piceoid* pits (Fig. 74c) are similar to cupressoid pits in being bordered along two sides, but the apertures are characteristically extended and almost linear in outline. They occur in *Picea*, *Pseudotsuga*, *Larix* and certain other genera.

(d) *Pinoid* pits (Fig. 74d) are small, simple pits, variable in outline and found in a number of pines.

(e) *Taxodioid* pits (Fig. 74e) differ from the other types in that they are included, i.e. the tracheid walls slope outwards from the outer aperture to an inner aperture that is larger than the pit. The outer aperture is usually small and elliptical in outline. These pits can be found in *Taxodium*, *Abies*, *Thuja*, *Cedrus* and certain other genera.

Intermediate forms of these pit types occur in many softwoods.

While the radial walls of the tracheids are pitted when in contact with rays, the tangential walls are also often modified close to rays, being thicker [82].

Fig. 79. Uniseriate rays built up of thin walled ray parenchyma cells in *Pinus maritima* Poir (Pinaceae). Note the intercellular spaces (IS). TLF × 250.

Fig. 80. A uniseriate ray built up of ray parenchyma cells with slightly thickened walls and small intercellular spaces in *Pseudotsuga menziesii* Franco (Pinaceae). Note the tracheid to ray cross field pitting and the simple pits in the ray cells. TLF × 850.

Fig. 81. A part biseriate ray in *Sequoia sempervirens* Endl. (Taxodiaceae). TLF × 400.

Fig. 82. Ray cell (R) to tracheid (T) simple pitting (arrowed) in *Cedrus atlantica* Manetti (Pinaceae). Note also the ray cell to intercellular space blind pit. TLF × 2700.

Fig. 83. Simple pits in thickened end walls of ray parenchyma cells give the walls a nodulated appearance. This is part of a ray in *Larix decidua* Mill. (Pinaceae). RLF × 1300.

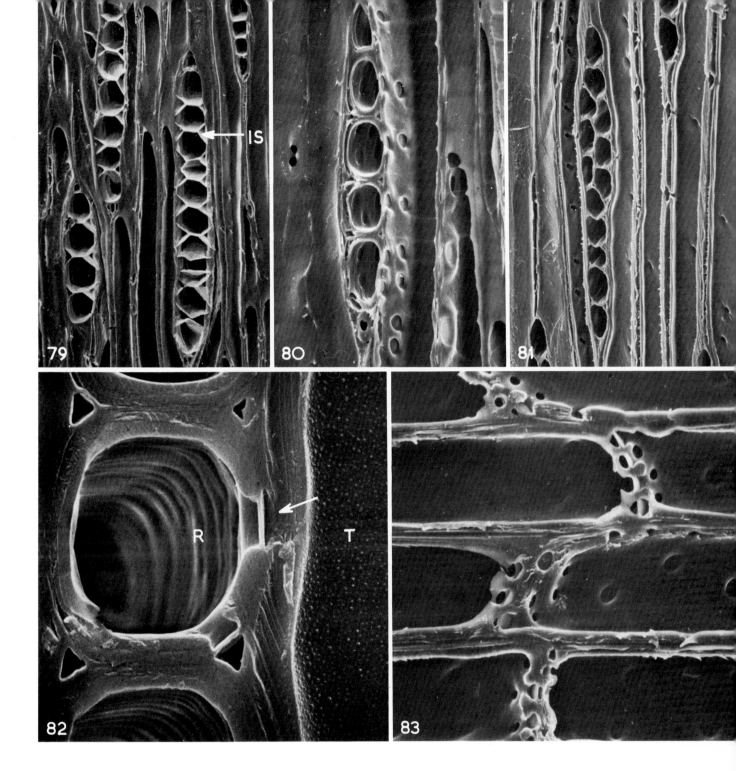

2.3 Tracheid wall thickenings

Helical or spiral thickenings overlaid on the S$_3$ layer (*see* Section 1.3) are known to occur as a regular feature of the axial and ray tracheids of *Pseudotsuga* (Figs. 75 and 86), *Taxus* (Figs. 76 and 103), *Torreya*, *Cephalotaxus* and *Amentotaxus* [131]. In *Pseudotsuga*, the helical thickenings are most conspicuous in the earlywood tracheids, but are sometimes absent in the latewood. In *Taxus* and *Torreya* the helical thickenings commonly occur throughout the growth ring. They also occur in the latewood axial tracheids of *Picea smithiana* [75], occasionally in the latewood of some other *Picea* species and in the latewood tracheids of a number of other genera including *Larix* [37].

The helical cavities found in the S$_2$ layer and so characteristic of compression wood tracheids (*see* Section 2.8) are not a form of helical thickening, nor are the splits that sometimes occur on drying especially in cells having a large S$_2$ microfibril angle (Fig. 77). Such checkings can sometimes be confused with helical thickening during superficial examination.

In some species of *Callitris*, and also in *Dacrydium cupressinum* and certain other woods, localized thickenings are sometimes found on top of the S$_3$ layer of the radial walls of tracheids close to the bordered pits. This form of thickening is termed *callitrisoid thickening* (Fig. 78).

A third form of wall thickening, termed *crassulae* and found exclusively on the radial walls of axial tracheids, may result from localized thickening of the middle lamella and primary walls close to intertracheid pits.

2.4 Rays

The arrangement of cells into axial and ray systems is a characteristic of all gymnosperm woods. While the axial system is built up predominantly of tracheids and some axial parenchyma cells, the ray system is built up largely of ray parenchyma cells with ray tracheids present in some woods. The rays of most softwoods are uniseriate, i.e. only one cell wide (Figs. 53, 54, 79 and 80), although some part *biseriate* rays, i.e. those that are two cells wide for part of their height, can usually be found (Fig. 81). Fully biseriate rays are unusual in all but a few softwoods [56]. Ray height, that is, the number of cells in vertical extent also varies with species. In most softwoods rays up to 15 cells high can be found. The highest rays, sometimes in excess of 60 cells high, have been found in *Sequoia sempervirens*.

Ray parenchyma cells generally have primary walls only, but secondary thickening can occur in some species (Figs. 80 and 82) especially in heartwood [7]. They are the only cell type present in the rays of many softwoods. If the wall thickening is sufficient to produce pitting,

Fig. 84. Ray tracheids (lower two rows of cells) and ray parenchyma cells (upper rows) from a ray in *Picea pungens* Engelm. (Pinaceae). Ray tracheid to axial tracheid and ray tracheid to ray tracheid pits are similar to the pits between contiguous axial tracheids being of the conifer raised border type. Note the light helical thickenings, a feature of the latewood tracheids of this species. RLF × 2100.

Fig. 85. Dentate thickenings in ray tracheids of *Pinus radiata* D.Don (Pinaceae). (Note the ray tracheid to ray tracheid conifer bordered pits (arrowed). The row of cells to the top are ray parenchyma). RLF × 1500.

Fig. 86. Helical thickenings in a ray tracheid (upper cell) of *Pseudotsuga menziesii* Franco (Pinaceae). RLF × 1600.

Fig. 87. A multiseriate ray in *Pinus maritima* Poir. (Pinaceae). Multiseriate rays are rare in softwoods. When present they usually contain a resin canal ensheathed in thin walled epithelial cells. TLF × 300.

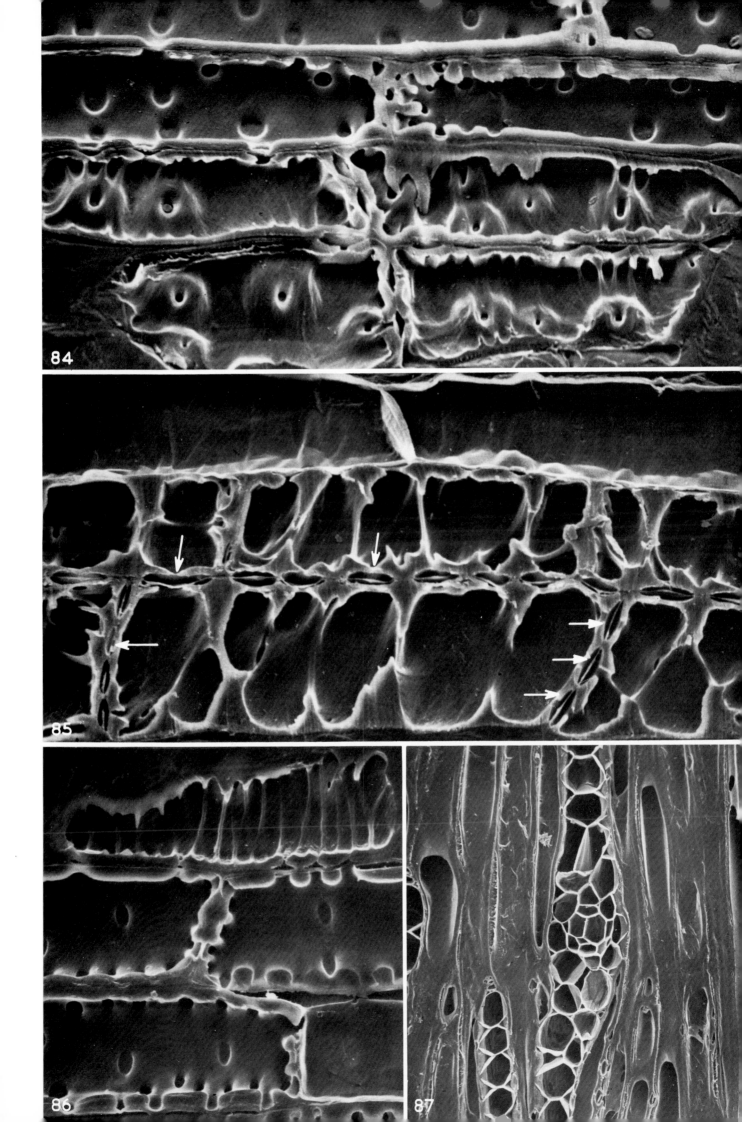

then the pits are usually simple (Fig. 82). Sometimes, however, the walls are so thin that true pits are absent [89] (Figs. 18, 60 and 85). Ray parenchyma cells are usually pitted on their radial walls. In some softwoods, e.g. *Tsuga*, *Picea* and *Abies*, prolific pitting of the end (tangential) walls may give the appearance of nodules (Fig. 83). In some woods the upper and lower (transverse) walls may also be pitted (Figs. 84 and 86).

Ray tracheids as well as parenchyma cells are present in the rays of a number of woods including *Pinus*, *Picea*, *Larix*, *Pseudotsuga* and *Tsuga*. In the last four of these genera they are usually confined to the upper and lower margins of the ray, but in *Pinus* they are more common and may constitute the entire ray in the smaller rays of the hard pines. Ray tracheids can be distinguished from ray parenchyma cells by the presence of conifer bordered pits. Rays built up entirely of ray tracheids are also a feature of *Chamaecyparis nootkatensis* [122]. They can also develop in other softwoods, apparently as a result of injury. Ray tracheids are similar to axial tracheids having thickened walls and bordered pits (Figs. 70, 84 and 85). Their end (tangential) walls are not pointed, however. Irregular depositions analogous to helical thickenings project from the walls of the ray tracheids of some hard pines. As they appear tooth-like in thin section such cells are said to be dentate (Fig. 85). In *Pseudotsuga*, helical thickenings are usually present (Fig. 86).

Softwoods with radial resin canals have some of their rays modified. These rays, which bear the resin canals, are sometimes called *fusiform rays* because of their appearance in tangential outline. Most fusiform rays contain only one resin canal located near the centre of the ray, but two resin canals per ray can occur in some pines. Fusiform rays are multiseriate near the canal (Figs. 53, 87 and 98). Their number rarely exceeds one twentieth of the total ray count. Radial resin canals develop in the same way as axial resin canals (*see* Section 2.7). The epithelial cells are thin walled in *Pinus* (Fig. 87) and thick walled in *Picea*, *Larix* (Fig. 98) and *Pseudotsuga* [122].

2.5 Axial parenchyma

While the axial cell system of softwoods is built up largely of non-living water conducting tracheids, two types of axial parenchyma cells can also occur in some woods. These cells differ from the tracheids in having thinner walls and a protoplast that often lives for many years. Some of these are elongated cells similar to the ray parenchyma cells but orientated axially instead of transversely and termed *longitudinal* or *wood parenchyma*. The others are resin excreting cells associated with axial resin canals and are termed *epithelial parenchyma*.

Longitudinal parenchyma is never common in softwoods. It can be found in most growth rings of *Taxodium*, *Chamaecyparis*, *Thuja*, *Libocedrus*, *Cupressus*

Fig. 88. Axial parenchyma cells (arrowed), containing starch grains, seen in a transverse face of *Dacrydium cupressinum* Lamb. (Podocarpaceae). The parenchyma cells are thinner walled than the adjacent tracheids. TF × 420.

Fig. 89. Axial parenchyma cells arranged in vertical strands in *Dacrydium cupressinum*. The horizontal cross walls are a consequence of the segmentation of fusiform cambial cells into a number of parenchyma cells. RLF × 420.

Fig. 90. The end walls of two contiguous axial parenchyma cells (P) in *Cryptomeria japonica* (L.f.) D.Don (Taxodiaceae) appear nodulated due to the pit-pairs and irregular wall thickening. RLF × 3000.

Fig. 91. Simple pits in the axial parenchyma cells of *Sequoia sempervirens* Endl. (Taxodiaceae) pairing with bordered pits in the tracheid walls to form half-bordered pit-pairs. RLF × 1400.

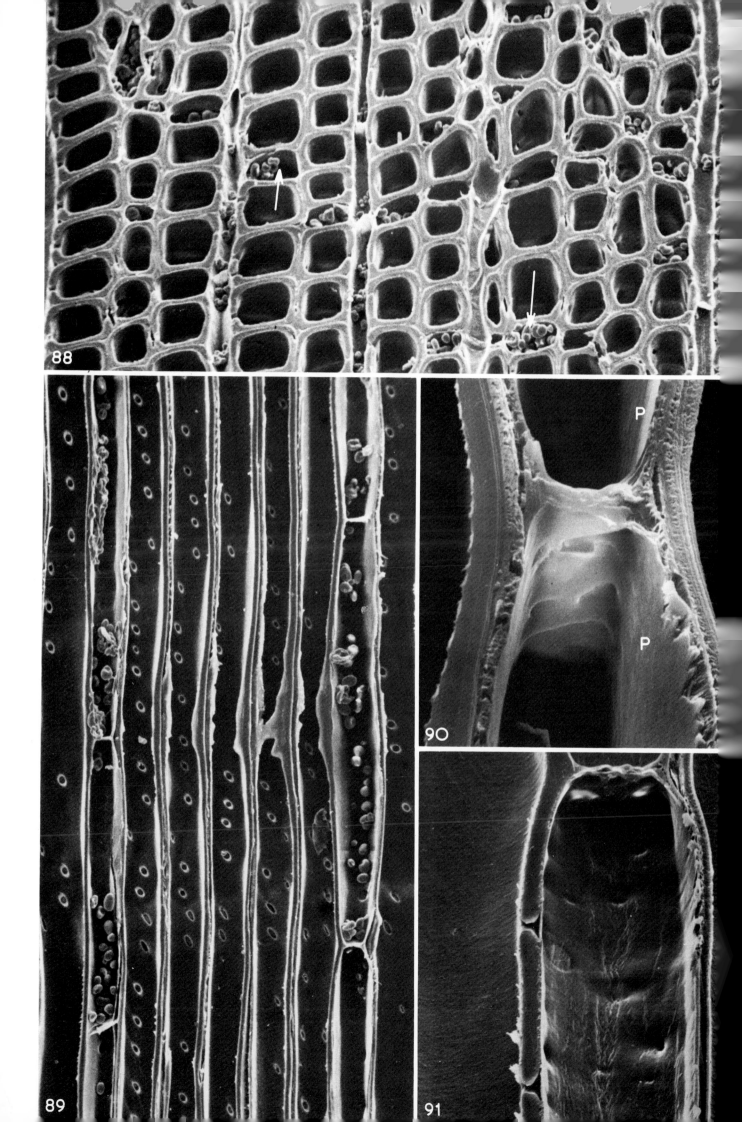

88

89

90

P

P

91

and *Sequoia* [37, 122] and is sometimes present in *Pseudotsuga*, *Tsuga*, *Larix*, *Podocarpus* and *Abies*. It is absent from *Taxus*, *Pinus*, *Picea* [122] and most *Dacrydium* sp. The individual cells are mostly solitary when viewed in the transverse plane (Fig. 88), but may be grouped into concentric bands. Axially they are usually arranged in columns or strands (Fig. 89), the end cells of each strand possessing pointed tips. The thickness of the cell wall varies, but is never as great as the tracheid walls. The end walls of most cells in a strand are transverse and when thickened, may appear to be nodulated (Fig. 90). The longitudinal parenchyma to tracheid or ray cell pits are usually simple with intact pit membranes (Fig. 91).

Longitudinal parenchyma cells commonly contain resin which may line the cell lumen or occur in discrete lumps on the walls or even appear to almost fill the cell (Fig. 52). For this reason they are sometimes called *resin cells*.

2.6 Strand tracheids

Cells resembling longitudinal parenchyma, but with thickened walls and bordered pits can be found in some softwoods. These cells often occur close to axial resin canals or within a parenchyma strand and are termed *strand tracheids* (Figs. 92 and 93). They arise by the segmentation of a fusiform cambial derivative by a number of cross walls and are therefore shorter than normal tracheids and have transverse end walls. The pits which occur on the end walls as well as the radial longitudinal walls are the same as normal intertracheid bordered pits (Fig. 93) with centrally thickened pit membranes. Some of the pits on the radial walls are large apertured strand tracheid to ray cell pits (Fig. 93). Strand tracheids have no living contents and appear to function in conduction. It has been suggested that they represent an intermediate state between the normal tracheids and longitudinal parenchyma cells. In the latewood of *Larix* and *Pseudotsuga* they sometimes replace parenchyma. They can also occur in or near traumatic tissue.

2.7 Resin canals

Many softwoods contain a dark coloured gummy substance called *resin*. Resin is a complex mixture and its chemical composition varies considerably from one species to another. It can occur either within wood cells (*intracellular*) or between cells (*intercellular*).

Intracellular resin occurs mainly in axial (Fig. 52) and ray parenchyma cells because resin formation is dependent on the cell having a living protoplast. It does occur occasionally in the tracheids of some woods, however, where it may appear as lumps on the walls or as biconcave discs known as *resin plates* (Figs. 94 and 95). Tracheids which contain resin are a feature of the woods

Fig. 92. Strand tracheids (arrowed) close to a resin canal in *Pinus radiata* D.Don (Pinaceae). Note the solitary trabecula to the lower left. RLF × 230.

Fig. 93. Detail of strand tracheids in *Pinus radiata* showing interstrand tracheid conifer bordered pits and strand tracheid to ray cross field pits. RLF × 1200.

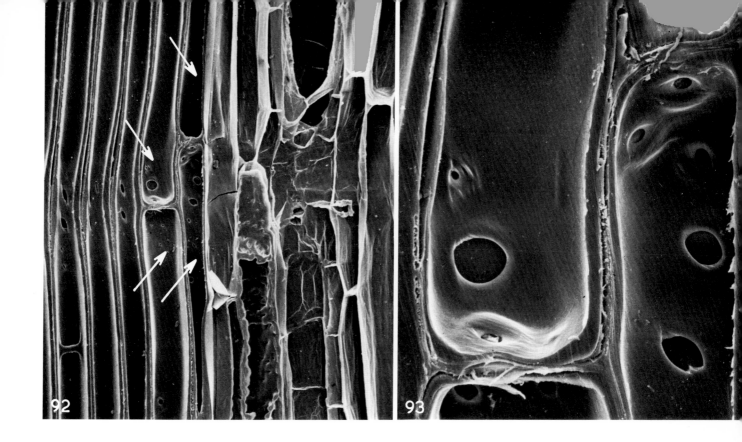

of *Agathis* and *Araucaria* where the resin plates usually form close to the rays.

Intercellular resin is found in axial and radial *resin canals* or *ducts*. Resin canals occur in most *Pinus, Pseudotsuga, Picea* and *Larix* woods. They develop by the formation of a canal within strands of thin walled parenchyma cells termed *epithelial cells* (Figs. 92 and 96). These cells exude resin into the cavity produced by their separation and usually surround the canals, forming an *epithelium*. Axial resin canals are usually more or less circular in transverse outline and solitary (Fig. 97), though they can occur in pairs in *Pseudotsuga*. Radial or transverse resin canals (Figs. 87 and 98) tend to be more irregular in outline. Epithelial cells which excrete resin are usually thin-walled, but in *Pseudotsuga, Picea* and *Larix* (Fig. 98), they have thick walls often profusely pitted. In *Pinus*, they become thick-walled in the heartwood due to the deposition of a secondary wall. Heartwood resin canals can also become filled with outgrowths developed from the epithelial cells, termed *tylosoids* [5] because of their similarity to tyloses (*see* Section 4.9). Tylosoids can also develop thickened walls.

While axial and radial resin canals are a normal feature of certain genera, *traumatic* or wound resin canals can develop in other genera not normally possessing such structures. Traumatic resin canals are usually confined to the earlywood and occur in tangential groupings.

Larger resin filled cavities sometimes lie in circumferential lens shaped pockets along the line of shakes and splits. Such cavities are often found along growth ring boundaries in trees grown in drought or high wind conditions. While their development is not fully understood, they are often caused by injury and must also be regarded as traumatic.

2.8 Compression wood

Compression wood is modified wood found to the lower side of leaning branches and trunks in some gymnosperms [160]. It is usually accompanied by an eccentric growth of the stem. It is found in members of the Ginkgoales, Coniferales and Taxales but it is not present in the Cycadales or Gnetales [162]. It develops as a reaction response to gravity or possibly stress [16] and apparently exerts sufficient force to maintain branches at their predetermined angle to the main axis. It can also restore a young stem to its vertical position following partial windthrow or avalanche damage.

Well developed compression wood is usually characterized by a reddish colour. The growth rings are wider than those in the normal wood and the contrast between the earlywood and latewood tracheids is reduced. The tracheids throughout the growth ring are more rounded in cross-section and thicker walled than those in normal wood, and intercellular spaces are common, especially in the earlywood (Figs. 99 and 100). Intercellular spaces are

Fig. 94. Resin plates (arrowed) forming 'false septa' across tracheids in *Agathis australis* Salisb. (Araucariaceae). Resin plates frequently form close to rays as in this micrograph, and may appear similar to the septa that sometimes divide hardwood fibres. The small cupressoid tracheid to ray crossfield pitting indicates the approximate extent to the ray. RLF × 1000.

Fig. 95. Resin plates (arrowed) close to a small ray in *Agathis australis*. TLF × 1400.

Fig. 96. Thin walled epithelial parenchyma cells lining an intercellular resin canal in *Pinus radiata* D.Don. (Pinaceae). RLF × 350.

Fig. 97. Thin walled epithelial cells surrounding a resin canal in *Pinus patula* L. (Pinaceae). TF × 350.

Fig. 98. A transverse or ray resin canal in *Larix decidua* Mill. (Pinaceae). The epithelial cells in this species have thickened walls. TLF × 1150.

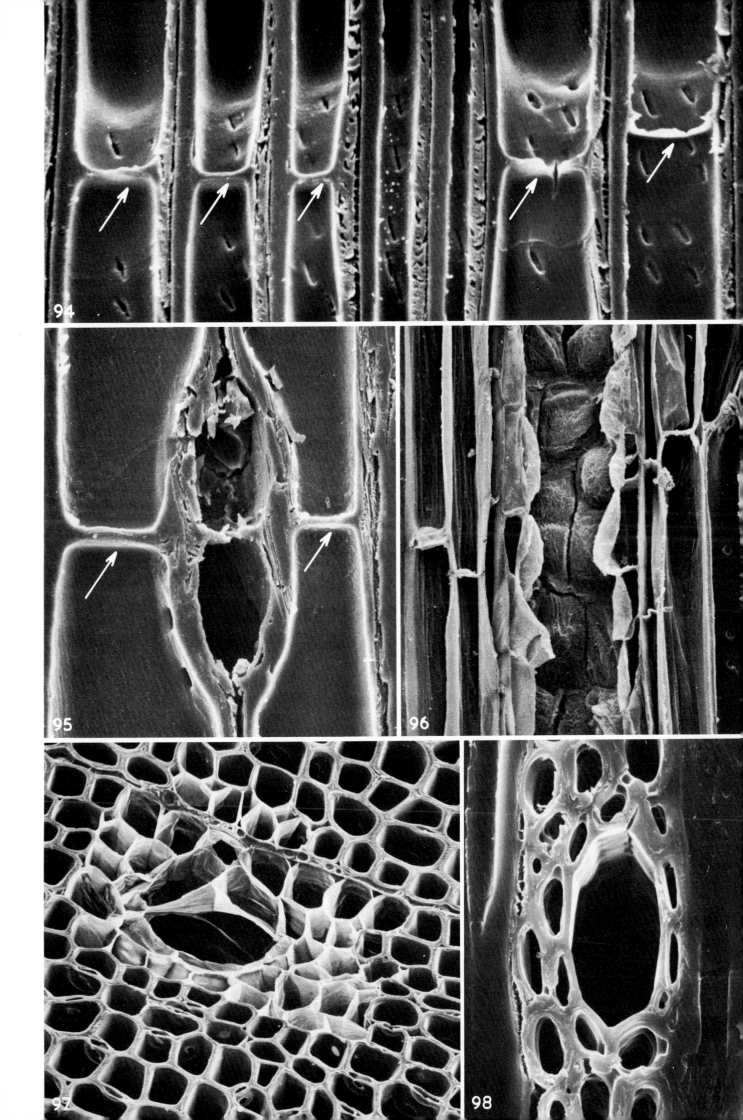

94

95

96

97

98

also reportedly a feature of the normal woods of some species of *Juniperus* [37, 88] and *Cupressus* (Fig. 101).

Compression wood tracheids generally lack an S_3 wall layer and the microfibril angle in the S_2 layer is larger than that in normal wood. Whereas S_2 microfibril angles of $10-20°$ can be expected in normal wood tracheids, those in compression wood tracheids approach $45°$. The S_1 layer is usually much thicker than in normal wood tracheids. The S_2 layer in compression wood tracheids also differs from that found in normal wood tracheids in frequently having helical cavities (Fig. 99). When viewed from the cell lumen, the wall surface may, as a consequence, appear faintly ribbed (Figs. 99 and 104). This gives a reliable indication of the angle of the S_2 microfibrils. There is a tendency for some of the cavities to open up during drying into large splits or checks often continuous with the pit apertures. Compression wood has a lower cellulose and a higher lignin content than normal wood [39, 130].

Some softwoods do not have all the anatomical modifications associated with typical compression wood in their leaning stems. Helical cavities for example, are not found in the Taxales, Ginkgoales or Araucariaceae [162]. Even in one species, grades of compression wood can be found where one or more of the 'typical' features are not consistently observed [62]. For instance intercellular spaces, generally regarded as a reliable guide to the presence of compression wood, are sometimes absent. A large microfibril angle for the S_2 layer, and to a lesser extent, the absence of the S_3 layer and a thicker S_1 layer are the most reliable indications of the presence of compression wood.

Some softwoods that feature helical thickenings on the lumen surfaces of their normal wood tracheids also have helical thickenings present in their compression wood tracheids. In the compression wood tracheids of both *Taxus baccata* L. and *Torreya californica* Torrey, the helical thickenings, possibly as a consequence of the absence of the S_3 layer, follow the microfibril angle of the S_2 layer (Fig. 103) rather than the almost transverse orientation of the S_3 wall layer present in normal wood tracheids [161] (Fig. 76). Helical thickenings are generally absent in the compression wood tracheids of *Pseudotsuga menziesii* Franco [161] (Fig. 104). When present, the warty layer may overlie the S_2 layer in much the same way as it would the S_3 layer (Fig. 102) in a normal wood tracheid.

Compression wood is a serious defect in timber. Although it has a higher density than normal wood, it is structurally much weaker. It has a lower tensile strength, modulus of elasticity and impact strength than normal wood. Its longitudinal shrinkage may be as high as 7 per cent whereas normal wood exhibits negligible longitudinal shrinkage. Its tendency to break suddenly under tensile load renders it almost useless as a structural material. It also has inferior paper making properties.

Fig. 99. Compression wood in *Pinus radiata* D.Don (Pinaceae) showing rounded tracheids with helical cavities in their cell walls. Note also the intercellular spaces. TF × 3500.

Fig. 100. Intercellular spaces in compression wood of *Cupressus macrocarpa* Gord. (Cupressaceae). TF × 750.

Fig. 101. Intercellular spaces in normal wood of *Cupressus macrocarpa*. TF × 750.

Fig. 102. A warty layer overlying the S_2 layer, including the helical cavities, of a compression wood tracheid in *Juniperus virginata* L. (Cupressaceae). RLF × 4500.

Fig. 103. Helical thickenings on the lumen surface of the S_2 layer in compression wood tracheids of *Taxus baccata* L. (Taxaceae). In compression wood the winding angle of the helical thickenings follows the steeper pitch of the S_2 microfibrils rather than the lower pitch characteristic of the S_3 layer as in normal wood tracheids (*see* Fig. 76). RLF × 2000.

Fig. 104. Normal wood (left) grading into compression wood (right) in *Pseudotsusa menziesii* Franco (Pinaceae). Helical thickenings are absent from the compression wood tracheids in this species but helical cavities in the S_2 layer are common. RLF × 650.

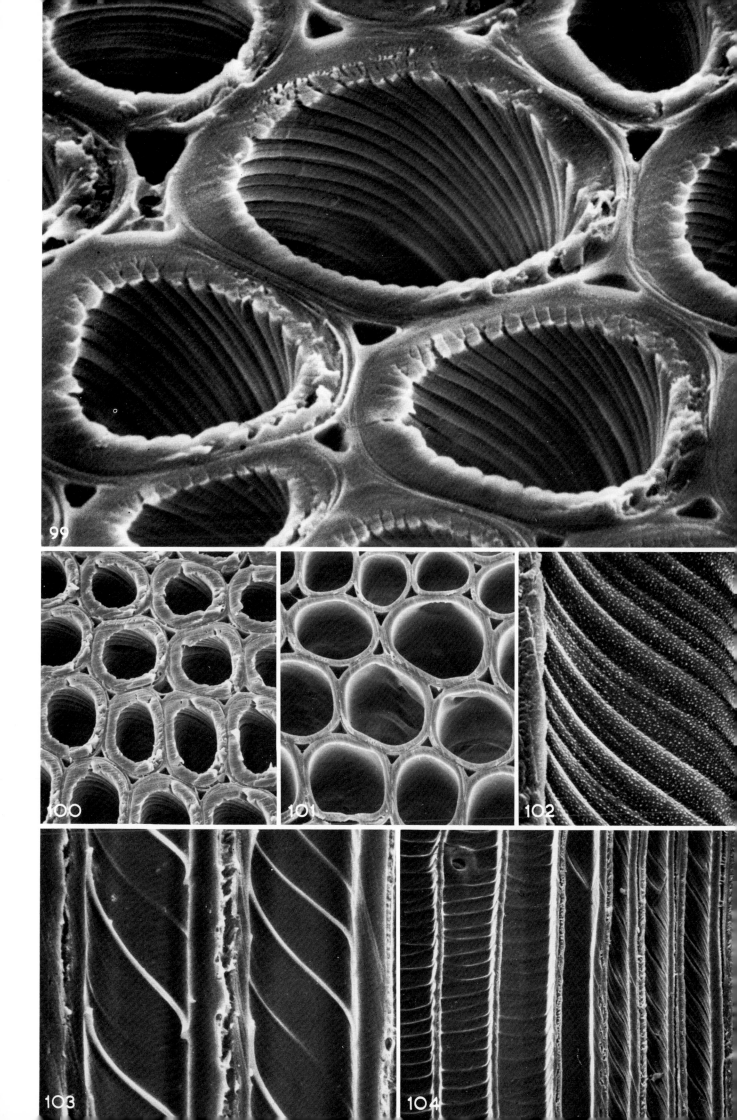

3 The Structure of palmwood

Although the monocotyledons of most temperate countries rarely achieve any great size, tree-like monocots with large, long-lived trunks are a conspicuous feature of many tropical floras. Although these plants do not produce 'wood' in the usual sense of the word, their stems are physically hard [83, 163], and can grow to 20 – 60 cm or more in diameter. The stems of the coconut palm (*Cocos nucifera L.*) are used extensively as a structural material in The Philippines.

In woody gymnosperms and dicotyledons, lateral growth originates in the vascular cambium so that the trunk increases in radius simultaneously with its axial growth [141]. Cell differentiation proceeds relatively quickly, with the cytoplasm dying and degenerating soon after the deposition of the secondary wall in most xylem cells. There is no further increase in cell dimensions or wall thickness. In palms, however, different growth processes occur. For the first few years the stem expands radially with little height growth and then, due to the activity of the apical meristem, all subsequent growth occurs in the axial direction with little further radial growth. There is no vascular cambium and most of the cell types present in the stem remain alive for a large part of the life of the palm. During this time anatomical changes continue to take place.

Palm stems comprise a large central core of primary vascular bundles embedded in a parenchymatous ground tissue (Figs. 105 and 106), surrounded by a cortex [163]. In some palms the density and texture of the central core of 'wood' varies greatly between different parts of the stem. The basic density decreases with increasing height in the stem and increases from the stem centre to the outside at any one height [94]. The typical range of basic density in *Cocos nucifera*, for example, is 100 – 900 kg/m^3 which is considerably greater than that found in any one softwood or hardwood. These changes result from differences in the distribution and size of the vascular bundles and variations in the thickness of the parenchyma and fibre walls. In most palms the vascular bundles are grouped much closer together in the peripheral zone (Figs. 105 and 108) than nearer the stem centre [163] (Figs. 105 and 107). The severity of this difference depends on the palm, being less marked in the coryphoid and scandent palms for example [136]. The denser outer region of the 'wood' clearly provides the main mechanical support for the palm and it is from this region that any timber used for structural purposes is usually cut [120].

An understanding of the three dimensional pathways traced out by the vascular bundles within the stem is fundamental to a full understanding of the structure of palmwood. Substantial progress towards our understanding of these complex vascular systems has been made in recent years using micro cine-photography of cut stems and microscope sections [182, 183]. Generally, the vascular bundles follow a shallow helix as they ascend the trunk and vary their distance from the stem centre according to a set pattern [163]. Each vascular bundle consists of xylem, phloem, axial parenchyma and fibres (Figs. 109 and 110). Non-vascular bundles composed of fibres only, are also present in some palms especially at higher levels near the stem centre (Figs. 111 – 113).

Fibres constitute over half the volume of each vascular bundle and give palm stems their axial strength. The percentage of the stem crossectional area that fibres occupy depends both on the position in the stem and also on the species. The vascular bundles in the peripheral zone of many palms are commonly capped by massive radially extended fibrous sheaths (Fig. 110). Because the vascular bundles are also more crowded near the periphery than nearer the stem centre (Fig. 108), the overall effect produces a stem with the greatest strength around the outside.

Generally, fibres have thin walls and large lumens near the stem centre (Figs. 109 and 114) and thick walls and small lumens near the stem periphery [83, 94] (Figs. 110 and 115). High up the stem the difference becomes less marked. The fibre walls are commonly multi-layered [126, 135] (Figs. 113 and 115). This layering is also clearly visible under both normal and polarised light microscopy. Each layer is believed to consist of two lamellae comparable in thickness and microfibril orientation to the S_1 and S_2 wall layers of conifer tracheids or hardwood fibres. A multi-layered palm fibre-wall is therefore built up of a series of repeating S_1 and S_2 type

Fig. 105. Transverse face of *Cocos nucifera* L. (Palmae). the 'wood' comprises vascular bundles (dark spots) embedded in a parenchymatous ground tissue. The bundles are closer together nearer the stem periphery than at the stem centre. The zone outside the 'wood' comprises the cortex phloem and leaf traces. TF × 0.9.

Fig. 106. Vascular bundles in *Cocos nucifera* embedded in parenchymatous ground tissue. Each bundle comprises one or more large metaxylem vessels surrounded by axial parenchyma cells, an area of phloem, and is capped with fibres. TF/TLF × 120.

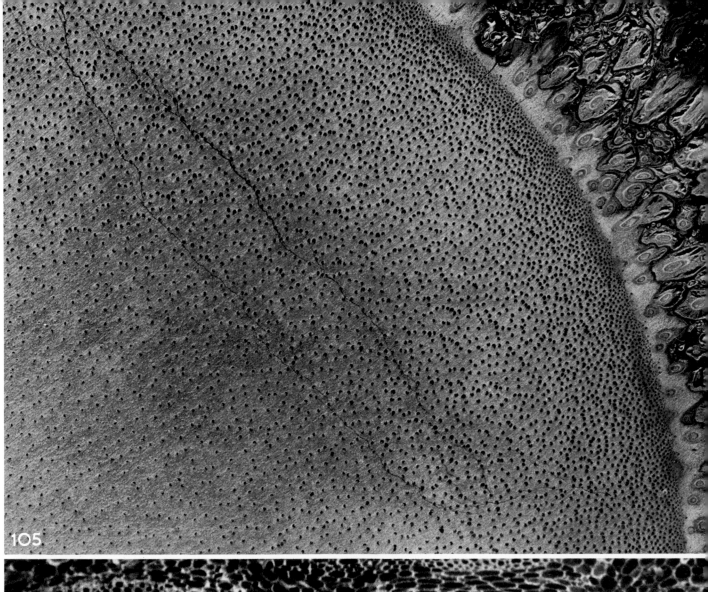

105

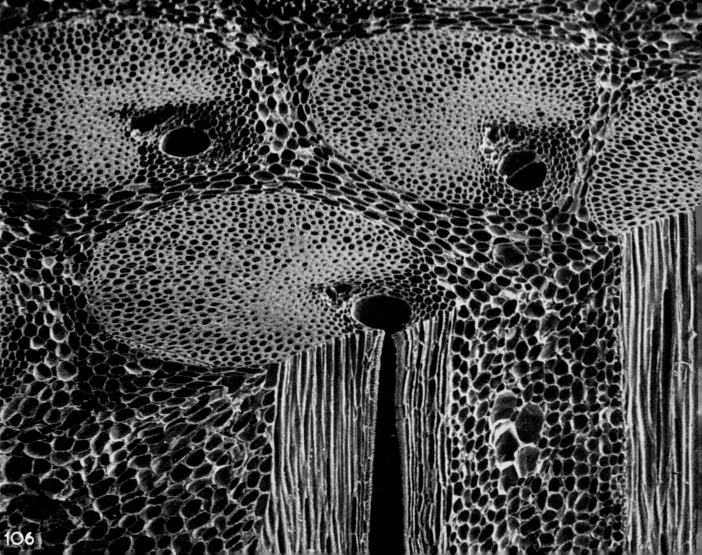

106

layers. The number of such repeating layers (and therefore the total wall thickness) is related to the age of the fibre. The presence of nuclei in palm stem fibres estimated to be several decades old, and the continued deposition of wall layers, are evidence of longevity of the fibre protoplasts.

Each vascular bundle also contains a number of tracheary cells that are characteristically *protoxylem*, and a number of larger *metaxylem* vessels nearer the phloem. If present, the protoxylem tracheary elements are generally tracheid-like cells, long with pointed tips, having thick secondary walls imperforate but interrupted by bordered pits often with scalariform apertures. Some metaxylem elements are also tracheid-like, but most bundles have at least one, and often several large vessels. In *Cocos* the vessel elements constituting the vessel are interconnected by predominantly simple perforation plates (Fig. 116) though some scalariform or part scalariform plates also occur (Fig. 117). Frequently there is an increasing specialization from the narrow early metaxylem vessel elements having oblique end walls with reticulate to many-barred scalariform perforation plates to the larger lumened vessel elements of the late metaxylem having transverse end walls with simple perforation plates. The wall pitting of most palm tracheary elements is scalariform (Fig. 118), but considerable variation in size occurs between equivalent pit types in different palms depending on the nature of the contiguous cell to which the vessel pit is forming the pit-pair.

Tyloses (*see* Section 4.9) occur frequently in the larger metaxylem vessels of many palms (Figs. 119 and 120). These structures are commonly close packed and have thickened walls interrupted by small pits.

Elongated axial parenchyma cells are also a feature of the vascular bundles of many palms (Fig. 121). These cells are usually closely associated with the vessel elements. Paratracheal parenchyma cells are thin walled with large simple pits and transverse end walls. Parenchyma cells further removed from vessels are thicker walled and have smaller pits.

A common feature of both the vascular and non-vascular bundles of many palms is the occurrence of silica-containing cells termed *stegmata*. Stegmata usually develop in longitudinal files adjacent to fibres [135]. They are similar to axial parenchyma cells but generally smaller. Fibres in contact with stegmata frequently have scalloped walls with the individual stegmata occupying each depression. Calcium oxalate crystals in the form of raphides are also common in the parenchyma cells of many palms (Figs. 123 – 125).

Each palm vascular bundle normally contains phloem sieve elements [132, 133, 134, 136, 137]. The cells are thin walled and contribute nothing to the mechanical strength of the stem. Mature sieve elements have a thin parietal cytoplasm but lack a nucleus. Their end walls are

Fig. 107. A transverse section near the centre of an old stem of *Cocos nucifera*. The vascular bundles are widely separated and the long-lived cells, particularly those in the fibre cap, are thick-walled. TF × 30.

Fig. 108. A transverse section from the peripheral zone of a young stem of *Cocos nucifera*. The vascular bundles are crowded together and the cells are relatively thin walled. TF × 30.

Fig. 109. Detail of a vascular bundle from a young stem of *Cocos nucifera*. Note the thin walled fibres. TF × 100.

Fig. 110. Detail of a vascular bundle from an older stem of *Cocos nucifera*. The fibres of the bundle cap have become very thick walled due to the deposition of additional secondary wall layers. Some thickening of the ground parenchyma cells is also evident. TF × 90.

Fig. 111. Non-vascular bundles scattered among the parenchymatous ground tissue near the stem centre in *Cocos nucifera*. TF × 80.

Fig. 112. Detail of the fibres in a non-vascular bundle from near the centre of a young stem in *Cocos nucifera*. TF × 425.

Fig. 113. Detail of the fibres in a non-vascular bundle from near the centre of an old stem of *Cocos nucifera*. Note the thick multi-layered fibre walls. TF × 550.

Fig. 114. Thin-walled fibres from the cap of a vascular bundle of *Cocos nucifera*. TF × 1300.

Fig. 115. Multi-layered thick-walled fibres from the cap of a vascular bundle of *Cocos nucifera*. Each wall layer is made up of a thin S_1 and a thicker S_2 type lamella. TF × 1900.

Figs. 111 to 115 are on page 52.

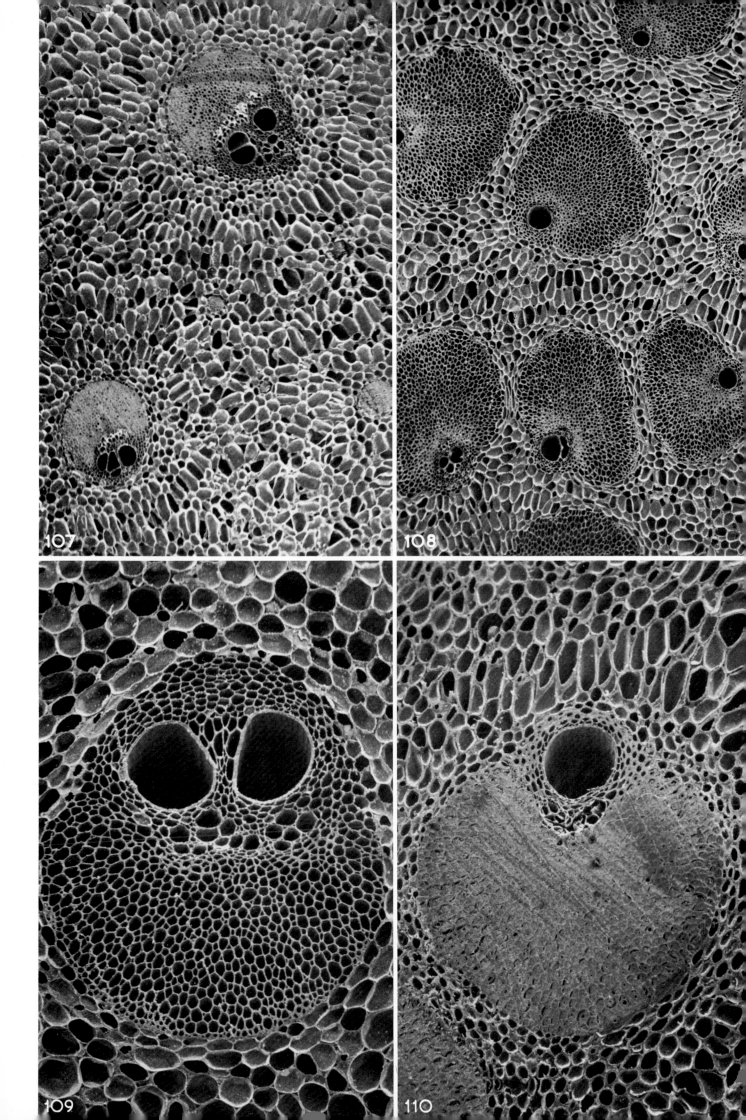

107

108

109

110

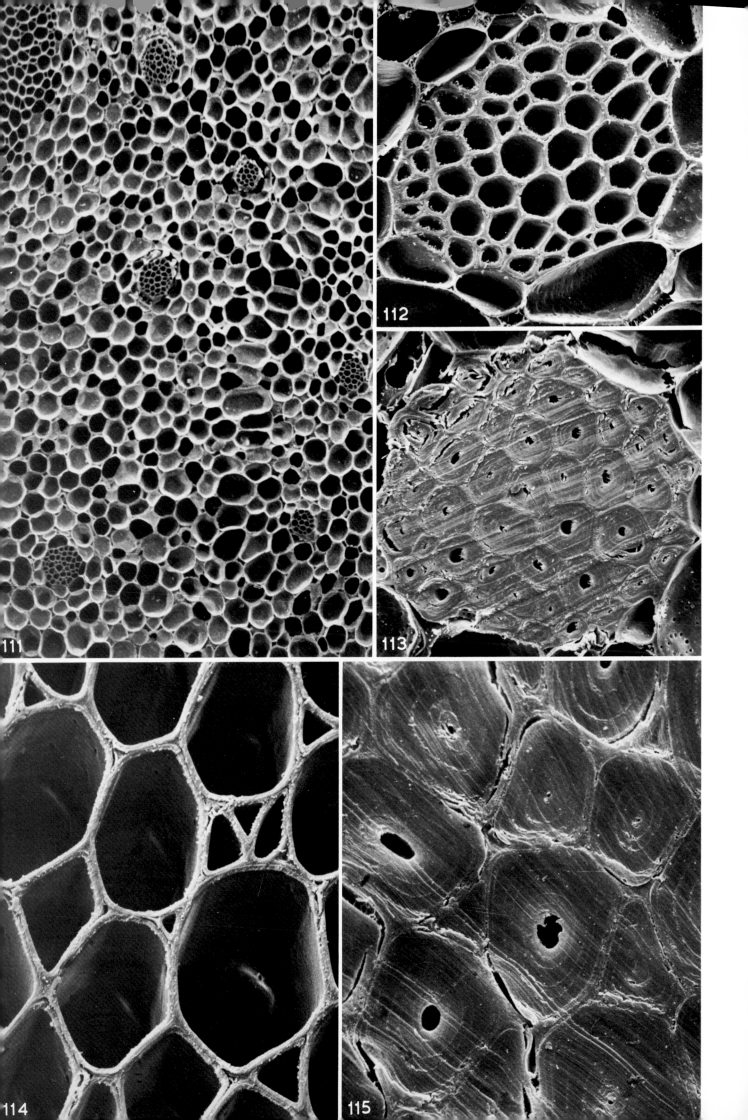

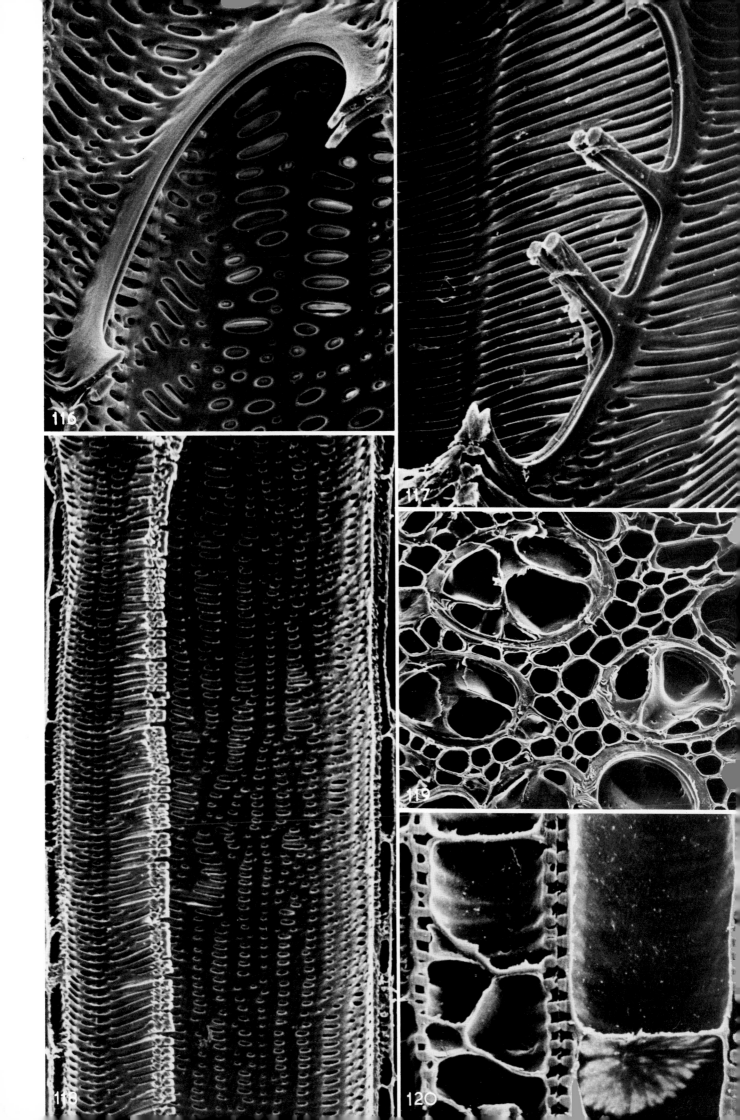

usually modified by the accumulation of sieve areas to form compound sieve plates (Fig. 122).

While the texture and density of a palm stem is largely dependent on the distribution of the vascular and non-vascular bundles, the proportion of fibres present in each bundle and the thickness of the fibre walls, changes occurring in the ground parenchyma tissue are also important [94]. Near the stem centre, the ground tissue consists mostly of spherical, thin walled cells with numerous large intercellular spaces (Figs. 126 and 128). With increasing distance from the stem centre, the walls of these cells become progressively thicker due to the deposition of further layers of wall material (Figs. 127 and 129). This does not occur in some cells possibly due to the early death of their cytoplasm.

An interesting feature of the ground tissue is the development of intercellular pectic strands [28] (Figs. 126 – 129). The amount of these appears to increase with the thickness of the adjacent cell walls.

The Monocotyledonae also contains the large tropical genus *Pandanus*. *Pandanus* wood, however, is softer than that of the palms and is of no commercial value. In addition to the palms and the pandans there are also a number of arborescent monocotyledons that show appreciable secondary growth in thickness from a specialized type of cambium. These include *Dracaena*, *Yucca* and *Cordyline*. Few of these, however, reach the size of the palms and none are abundant or dominant.

Fig. 116. A simple perforation plate connecting two metaxylem vessel elements in *Cocos nucifera*. RLF × 650.

Fig. 117. A scalariform perforation plate connecting two metaxylem vessel elements in *Cocos nucifera*. Note the long apertured intervessel scalariform pits. RLF × 550.

Fig. 118. Detail of the walls of two vessel elements in *Cocos nucifera* showing the scalariform intervessel pitting. RLF × 350.

Fig. 119. Close packed tyloses filling the vessel lumina of a vascular bundle of *Cocos nucifera*. Note the small inter-tylose pits. TF × 450.

Fig. 120. Tyloses in two adjacent vessels in *Cocos nuciferia*. Note again the intervessel pitting. The cells to the extreme left and right of this micrograph are axial parenchyma cells. RLF × 600.

Figs. 116 to 120 are on page 53.

Fig. 121. Axial parenchyma cells from a vascular bundle of *Cocos nucifera* (vessel wall to the right of the micrograph). The paratracheal parenchyma cells are very thin walled and have simple pits, while the parenchyma cells second and third out from the vessel have thicker walls and slightly bordered pits. RLF × 1200.

Fig. 122. A compound sieve plate between sieve tube elements of *Cocos nucifera* phloem. TF × 2600.

Figs. 123 – 125. Raphides in ground parenchyma cells of *Cocos nucifera*. × 625, × 700, × 1400 respectively.

Fig. 126. Thin walled ground tissue parenchyma cells from a young stem of *Cocos nucifera*. TF × 225.

Fig. 127. Thick walled ground tissue parenchyma cells from an old stem of *Cocos nucifera*. Note the pectic strands in the intercellular spaces. TF × 600.

Fig. 128. Detail of thin walled ground parenchyma cells from a young stem of *Cocos nucifera*. Note the pectic strands in the intercellular spaces. TF × 1450.

Fig. 129. Detail of thick walled ground parenchyma cells from an old stem of *Cocos nucifera*. Note the pectic strands in the intercellular spaces, the layering of the cell wall and the simple pit-pair (arrowed). TF × 1200.

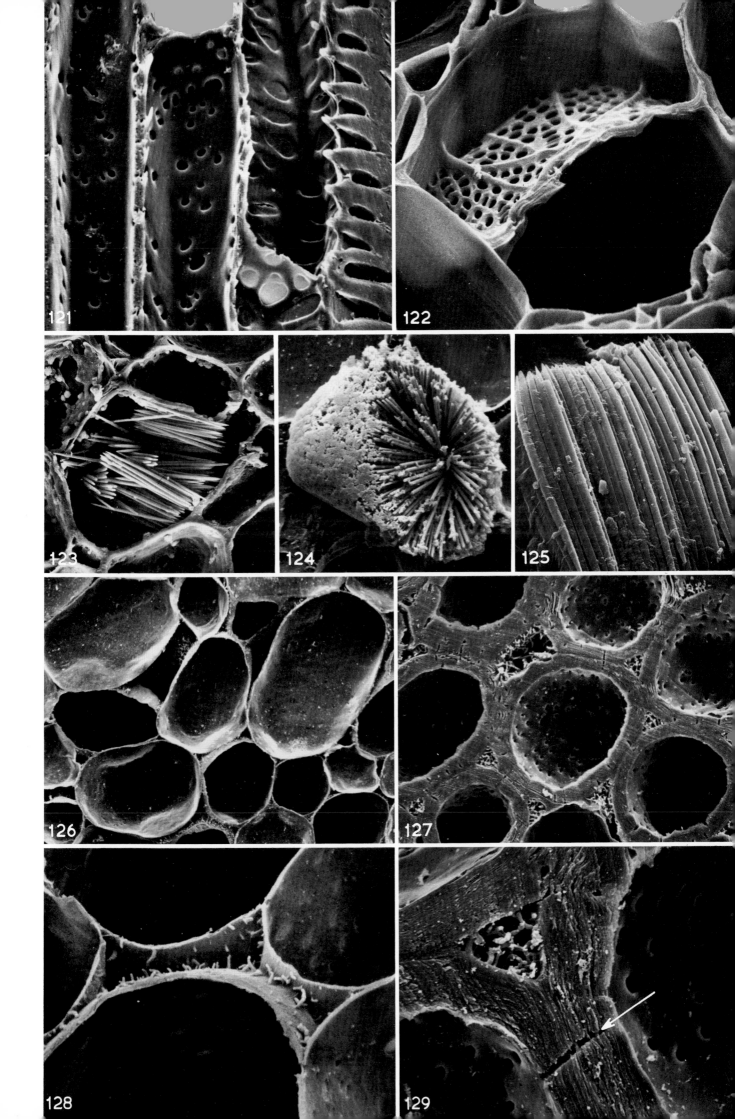

4 The Structure of hardwoods

The secondary xylem of dictotyledons is commonly called *hardwood* largely for historical reasons. It is considerably more complex than the wood of conifers because it contains a greater variety of cell types (Fig. 130). Whereas in softwoods the functions of conduction and support are performed by the one axial cell type – *the tracheid* – in most hardwoods these functions are carried out by different cell types. Vessels, built up of individual vessel elements joined end to end provide a pathway for the conduction of water and solutes up the trunk of the living tree, while long thick-walled fibres, variously grouped, function in support. Axial parenchyma cells are usually more abundant in hardwoods than in softwoods and the rays occupy a higher proportion of the wood volume with large multiseriate rays common in many species.

Hardwoods are also called *porous woods* because of the vessels or 'pores' which are sometimes visible to the naked eye in clean cut transverse faces. The grouping of these pores varies considerably from one species to another as does the diameter of the individual pores. In addition, the diameter of the pores of any one species usually varies within each growth increment.

Fibres of various types usually form the ground mass of the wood. They vary from long, thick-walled libriform fibres in some woods to somewhat less thick-walled and shorter fibre tracheids in others. Cells resembling narrow vessel elements, but lacking perforation plates are also found in some hardwoods. Known as *vascular tracheids*, these are thought to be incompletely developed vessels. Sometimes in the latewood a radial file of vessel elements may end with a number of narrow vascular tracheids. It is unlikely that these cells play a significant role in conduction.

Axial parenchyma is generally more prolific in hardwoods than in softwoods. The parenchyma cells are sometimes scattered throughout the ground mass (apotracheal), at other times they are closely associated with the vessels (paratracheal). Occasionally they are solitary, but usually they are grouped into aggregates. The occurrence of unusual forms of cambial activity in some hardwoods sometimes leads to the development of concentric bands of thin walled parenchyma.

Hardwoods normally have multiseriate rays. Although a number of woods exist with only uniseriate or uniseriate and part biseriate rays, by far the greater number of hardwoods have rays that are several cells wide. Sometimes these are only a few cells high, but in some instances they may extend the full length of the internode. Hardwood rays are sometimes flanked at the

Fig. 130. Transverse and tangential longitudinal faces of the porous hardwood *Magnolia grandiflora* L. (Magnoliaceae). The wood is built up of vessel elements interconnected by scalariform perforation plates and dense intervessel pitting, thin to moderately thick walled fibres, and multiseriate rays. Axial parenchyma is also present at the growth ring boundaries (not shown). TF/TLF × 180.

Fig. 131. Transverse and tangential longitudinal faces of the vessel-less dicot *Pseudowintera axillaris* (J. R. et G. Forst.) Dandy (Winteraceae). The wood is built up of tracheids, axial parenchyma and uniseriate and large multiseriate rays. TF/TLF × 210.

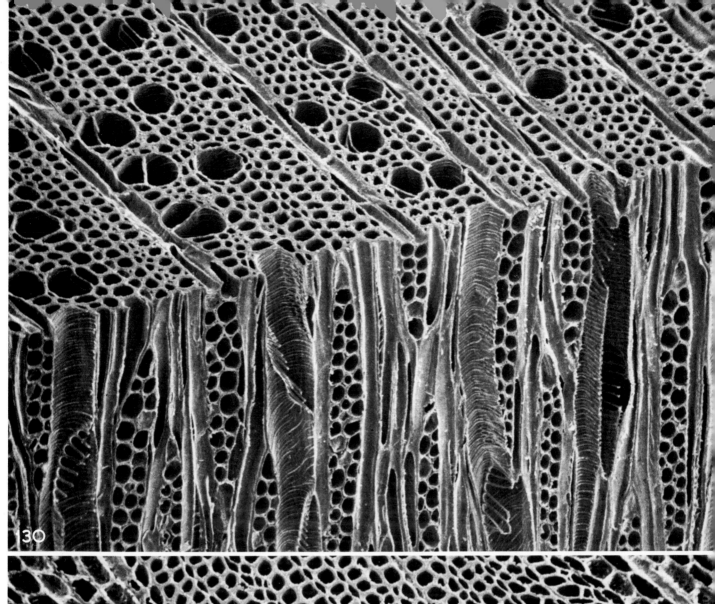

130

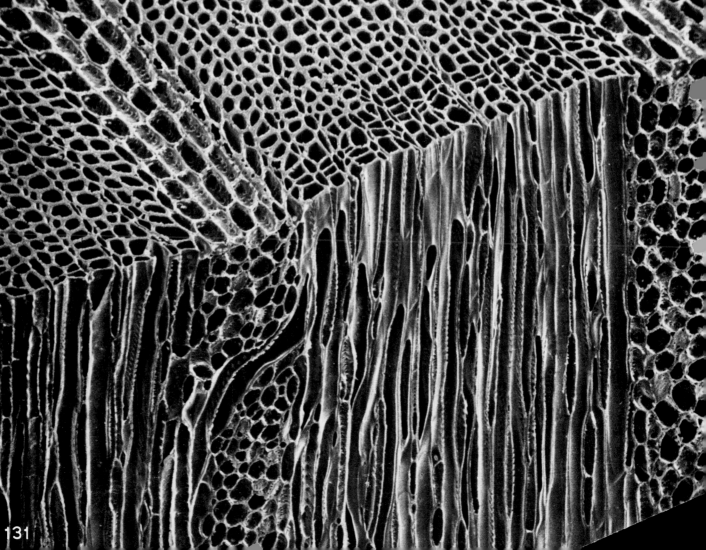

131

upper and lower extremities by modified cells and are sometimes enclosed by sheath cells. Radial conducting cells are absent.

While the presence of vessels marks the major distinguishing feature separating softwoods and hardwoods, it is important to note that there are a few exceptions to this rule. Vessels are lacking in the wood of a small number of dicotyledonous species belonging to three families. Such hardwoods are frequently referred to as the *vessel-less dicots* and their axial cell system is built up entirely of tracheids and axial parenchyma cells (Fig. 131). They can usually be distinguished easily from true coniferous woods by the presence of multiserate rays. Their tracheids also differ in being interconnected by bordered pit-pairs whose pit membranes lack a thickened torus.

4.1 Growth increments

The greater variety of cell types present in hardwoods means that more variation in cell arrangement within the growth ring is possible than in softwoods. Vessels may be of a similar diameter and distributed more or less evenly throughout the growth ring forming a *diffuse-porous* wood (Fig. 132), or may be much larger in the earlywood forming a *ring-porous* wood (Fig. 133). Many woods have a vessel arrangement that lies somewhere between these two extremes. For example, trees growing in many temperate climates and having vessels throughout each growth ring, tend to have larger lumened vessels in the earlywood grading down to smaller lumened vessels in the latewood (Fig. 134). Although some texts on wood anatomy describe such arrangements as *semi ring-porous* or *semi diffuse-porous*, in practice it is not always realistic to attempt to classify such intermediate forms. Additionally vessels are absent from the last few rows of cells in the latewood of almost all temperate trees.

Within each growth ring, the vessels may be *solitary* (Fig. 135) or grouped into *pore multiples*. Solitary vessels are a characteristic feature of certain families. Vessels forming pore multiples may lie in a *radial* arrangement (Fig. 136), form *pore clusters* (Figs. 137, 167 and 184) or be grouped into *tangential festoons* (Fig. 138).

Solitary vessels tend to be slightly oval in transverse section with the larger axis directed predominantly in the radial direction (Fig. 135). Vessels grouped in multiples tend to be angular in transverse outline (Figs. 136 and 137). Vessels also vary greatly in diameter from one wood to another. Small vessels may be of the order of 15 to 20 microns in diameter while the largest may be greater than 300 microns.

Fibres are generally found throughout the growth ring and in the latewood they may be thicker walled and have smaller lumens than in the earlywood (Fig. 169).

Fig. 132. Vessels distributed throughout the growth ring in the diffuse-porous wood *Pennantia corymbosa* J. R. et G. Forst. (Icacinaceae). A growth ring boundary is indicated. TF/RLF × 220.

Fig. 133. Large vessels in the earlywood of the ring-porous wood *Quercus robur* Liebl. (Fagaceae). The growth ring boundary is indicated. TF/RLF × 100.

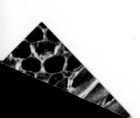

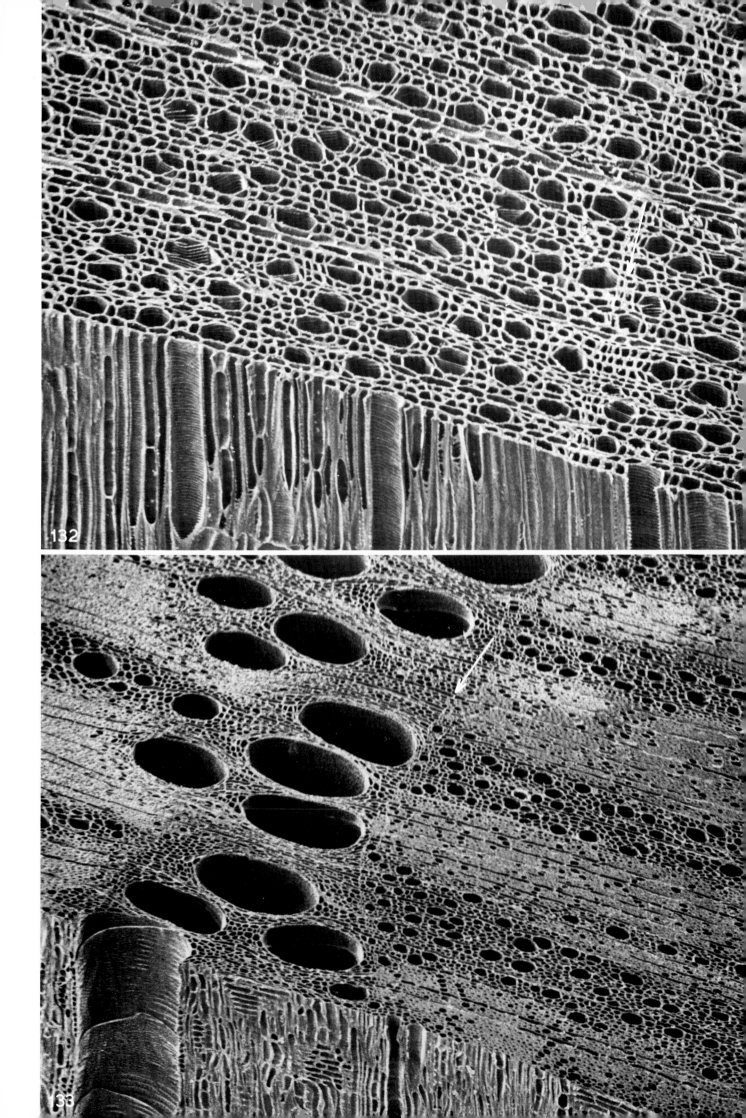

Axial parenchyma cells (described more fully in Section 4.6) can occur throughout the growth ring in a diffuse or diffuse-in-aggregates pattern, or they can be grouped into distinct bands. Sometimes banded parenchyma is *boundary* (Fig. 184), meaning that it occurs either in the latewood of one growth ring (*terminal*) or in the earlywood of the next (*initial*). Some woods are unusual in that they have a number of concentric bands of parenchyma within each growth ring. These can develop from the cyclic differentiation of the cambial derivatives first into vessel members, then into axial parenchyma and then into fibres, a number of times per growth ring (Fig. 138), or they may result from more unusual forms of cambial activity where a number of successive cambia develop (*see* Section 4.10). In the latter case, pockets of included phloem will also be present in the wood (Figs. 213 and 214).

Although not usually obvious in section or face views of wood, there is normally a progressive increase in the length of the cells from earlywood to latewood. This is greatest in the case of the fibres, but the transition also occurs between earlywood and latewood vessel elements and axial parenchyma strands (with the exception of those woods having a storeyed cambium (*see* Section 4.11)). These size changes result from seasonal changes in the length of the fusiform cambial initials in non-storeyed cambia. Vessel elements and axial parenchyma strands in woods with storeyed cambia, maintain a constant length both within each growth ring and also from the stem centre to the bark.

4.2 Vessel perforations

Sap moving through vessels passes relatively freely from cell to cell through perforations in the walls of the vessel elements. Perforations are virtually unobstructed openings in the end walls forming *perforation plates*. A perforation plate that consists of a single large opening is termed a *simple perforation plate* (Figs. 28, 36, 139 and 155). A number of openings grouped together form a *multiple perforation plate*. The openings in a multiple perforation plate can be arranged as a series of regular parallel slits separated by mainly unbranched dividing bars forming what is known as a *scalariform perforation plate* (Fig. 140), less regular shaped openings separated by dividing wall bars and arranged in an irregular or net arrangement form a *reticulate perforation plate* (Fig. 141), while a small number of large circular perforations grouped together form a *foraminate perforation plate*. Multiple perforation plates with regular and irregular perforations grouped in a manner ranging from scalariform to reticulate (Fig. 142) are usually described in a way that best reflects their nearest relationship [57]. A scalariform perforation plate with a few branched dividing bars but otherwise regular linear perforations is

Fig. 134. Vessels distributed throughout the growth ring, but larger in the earlywood of *Ulmus procera* Salisb. (Fagacaceae). Such a vessel arrangement is sometimes described as semi-ring porous. The growth ring boundaries are indicated. TF/RLF × 80.

Fig. 135. Solitary vessels in *Metrosideros umbellata* Cav. (Myrtaceae). TF × 100.

Fig. 136. Vessels arranged in radial files in *Elaeocarpus hookerianus* Raoul (Elaeocarpaceae). TF × 200.

Fig. 137. Vessels arranged in pore clusters in *Pseudopanax laetus* Philipson (Araliaceae). TF × 200.

Fig. 138. Vessels arranged in tangential festoons alternating with bands of fibres and axial parenchyma cells in *Plagianthus betulinus*, A. Cunn. (Malvaceae). TF × 150.

Fig. 139. A simple perforation plate between two vessel elements in *Knightia excelsa* R.Br. (Proteaceae). Note the pit membranes separating the intervessel pit-pairs in the side walls. RLF × 3000.

Fig. 140. Scalariform perforation plates between vessel elements in *Alnus glutinosa* (L.) Gaertn. (Betulaceae). Note the prolific intervessel pitting on the side walls of the vessel elements. RLF × 1650.

Fig. 141. A reticulate perforation plate between vessel elements of *Coprosma tenuicaulis* Hook.f. (Rubiaceae). Most of the perforation plates in this genus are simple but some multiple plates occur occasionally. RLF × 3100.

Figs. 139 to 141 are on page 62.

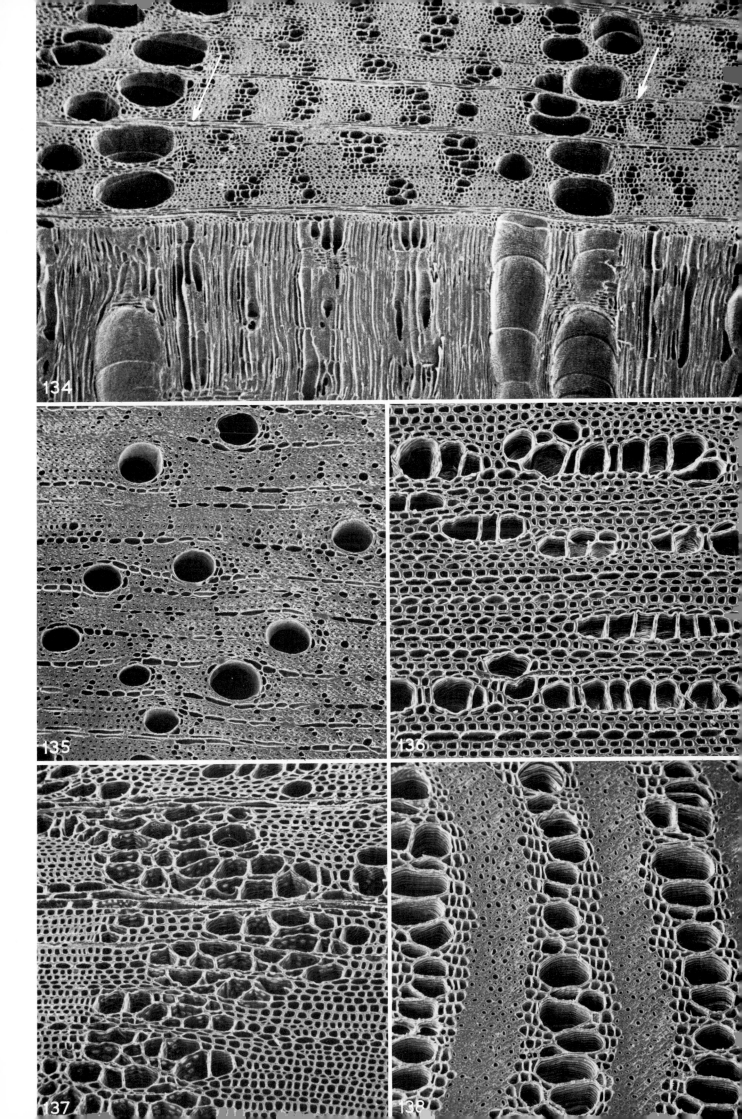

134

135

136

137

138

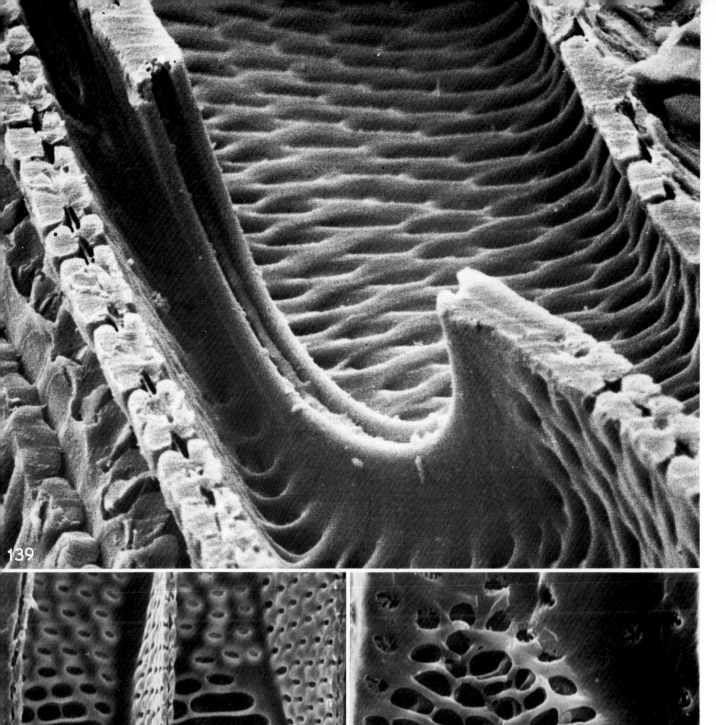

139

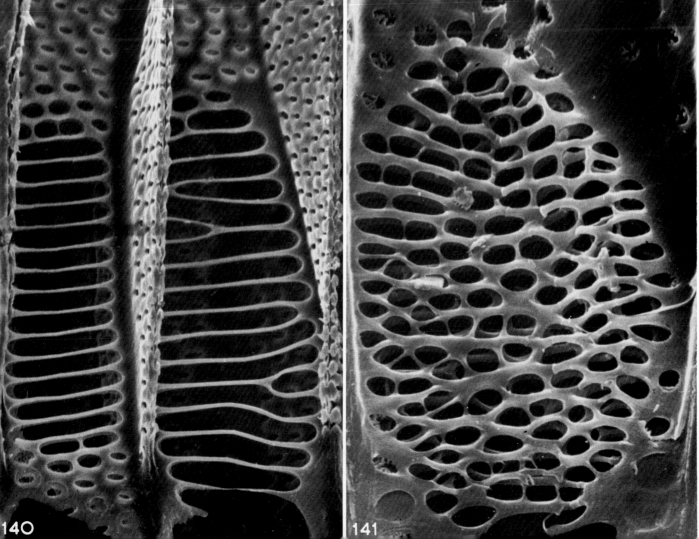

140

141

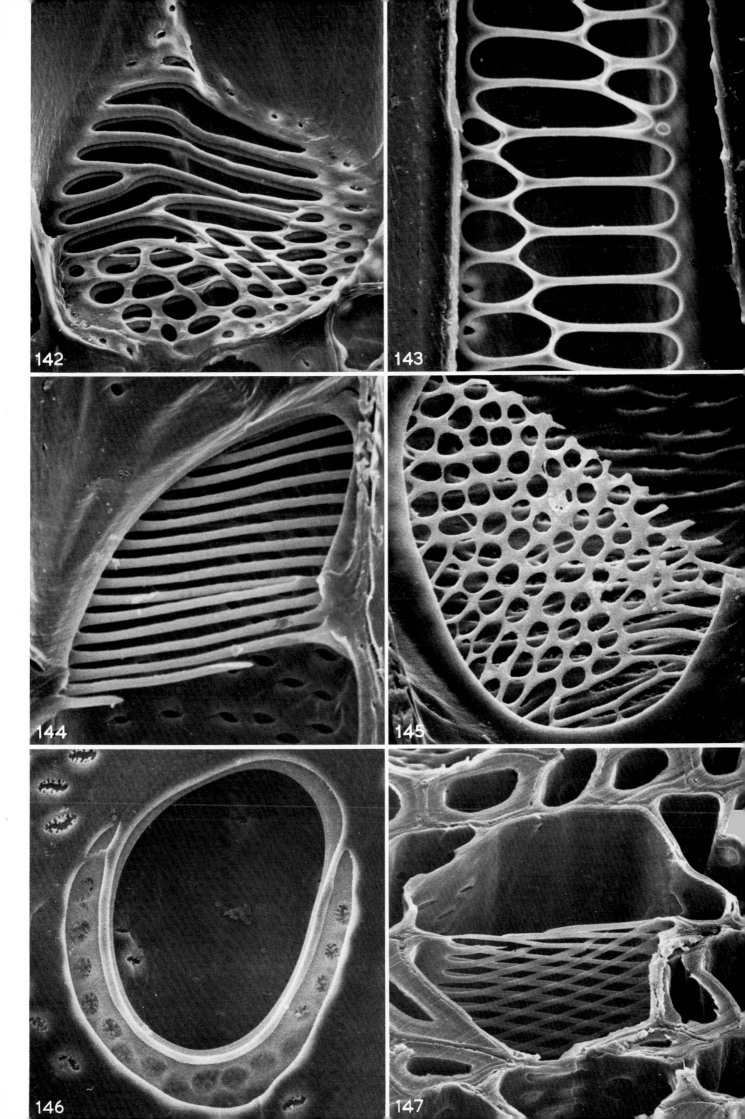

142

143

144

145

146

147

described as a *branched scalariform perforation plate* (Fig. 143). Perforation plates of complex and intermediate forms have been observed in numerous woods over the last decade using scanning electron microscopy [101, 117, 124].

Although many woods have exclusively simple or exclusively scalariform perforation plates between their vessel elements, there are a large number of woods that have more than one perforation plate type present. Where there is only one type of perforation plate, the openings in the walls of the adjacent cells normally coincide exactly in a simple to simple or scalariform to scalariform arrangement. However, where there is more than one type of perforation plate, the openings may not be coincident, and a single opening in the end wall of one vessel element may correspond with a series of scalariform or reticulate openings in the end walls of the adjacent vessel element. Such perforation plates are usually referred to as *combination or dimorphic perforation plates* [24, 99, 101]. Simple to scalariform (Fig. 144) combination perforation plates can occur in woods that have mostly simple perforation plates with a few scalariform or part scalariform plates, and also in woods with mostly scalariform perforation plates but also having a few simple perforation plates. Simple to reticulate combination perforation plates (Fig. 145) also occur in a number of woods but true scalariform to reticulate combination plates appear to be rare.

The occurrence of identical combination perforation plates in radial files of vessels has led to the suggestion that the tendency of a particular vessel element to produce a different type of plate in its end wall is determined by genetic factors transmitted to the daughter cells of each deviant fusiform cambial initial [24]. Despite the different arrangement of the openings in the end walls of adjacent vessel elements forming a combination plate, the total area of the perforation plate usually coincides exactly. The failure of one vessel element to produce a perforation opposite the opening in the wall of an adjacent vessel element leads to the formation of a *blind perforation* (Fig. 146). In rare instances the dividing bars in the multiple plates of adjacent cells may also mismatch. Where this occurs in an otherwise normal scalariform perforation plate, for example, a crossed perforation plate can result [101, 117] (Fig. 147).

Perforation plates develop during the differentiation of a column of vessel elements behind the cambium [20, 96, 115]. A secondary wall is deposited over the primary wall of each differentiating vessel element after the cell has reached its final size. The pits and areas to be perforated do not become overlaid with secondary wall though both may be overarched by prominent borders of wall material [117]. Perforation partitions (Figs. 148 and 149), composed of the primary walls of the adjoining cells and the intervening middle lamella in the area to be

Fig. 142. A part scalariform − part reticulate perforation plate between two vessel elements in *Platanus acerifolia* Willd. (Platanaceae). RLF × 1150.

Fig. 143. A branched scalariform perforation plate in *Hedycarya arborea* J. R. et G. Forst. (Monimiaceae). RLF × 1450.

Fig. 144. A simple to scalariform combination perforation plate in *Brachyglottis repanda* J. R. et G. Forst. (Compositae). RLF × 2200.

Fig. 145. A simple to reticulate combination perforation plate in *Coprosma arborea* Kirk (Rubiaceae). RLF × 2500.

Fig. 146. A blind perforation in a simple to multiple combination perforation plate in *Carmichaelia angustata* Kirk. RLF × 1700.

Fig. 147. A crossed perforation plate between two vessel elements in *Quintinia acutifolia* Kirk (Escalloniaceae). TF × 1650.

Figs. 142 to 147 are on page 63.

Figs. 148 to 153. Perforation plate development in *Knightia excelsa* R.Br. (Proteaceae) (Figs. 148, 150 and 152) a wood with simple perforation plates, and *Laurelia novae-zelandiae* A. Cunn. (Atherospermataceae) (Figs. 149, 151 and 153) a wood with scalariform perforation plates.

Figs. 148 and 149. Early development of simple and scalariform perforation plates. Secondary walls have covered the primary walls of the contiguous vessel elements except in the areas to be perforated. The perforation partitions are built-up of the primary walls of the adjacent cells and the intervening middle lamellae. RLF × 2200 and × 1750 respectively.

Figs. 150 and 151. The perforation partitions are subsequently removed by enzymatic action. RLF × 4800 and × 4700 respectively.

Figs. 152 and 153. Some cellulosic material usually survives the partition digestion process. Microfibrillar webs are very rare in simple perforation plates (152) but are quite common in scalariform ones where they may obstruct the corners of or even the entire opening in the last few openings in long plates. RLF × 2900, × 1600 respectively.

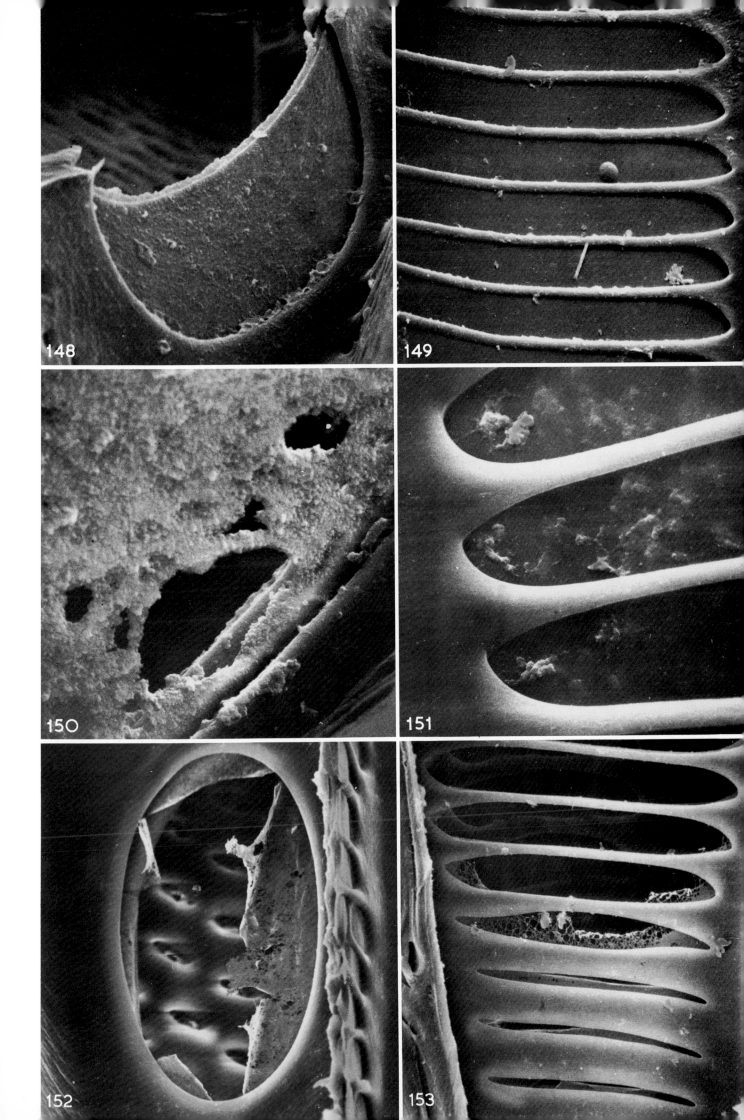

perforated, become slightly thickened possibly as a result of the swelling of the intercellular material. They are subsequently removed by enzymatic action (Figs. 150 and 151) [109, 110, 181]. Whether this action results from the presence of enzymes in the middle lamella and primary walls of the partition or by the action of cytoplasmic enzymes is still not clear. The perforation partition digestion process normally leaves the openings in simple perforation plates clear of obstructions. All that remains of the partition at cell maturity is a small ridge of material between the overarching secondary wall borders (Fig. 139) though in rare instances undigested microfibrillar fragments of the primary walls may remain [72, 93, 117, 127] (Fig. 152). In the smaller openings in multiple perforation plates, however, these microfibrillar webs are commonly found traversing the individual openings at each end of long scalariform perforation plates in fully differentiated vessel elements [93, 97, 158] (Fig. 153). It is possible in multiple perforation plates that these microfibrillar webs survive the initial enzymatic breakdown process only to be subsequently removed from most of the openings by the onset of the transpiration stream. Complete microfibrillar webs traversing every opening in scalariform perforation plates are usually found only in vessel elements close to the cambium [97] (Fig. 154).

The individual perforations in the vessel elements of most woods are usually prominently bordered with overarching rims of secondary wall material [117] (Fig. 139), though in some woods such borders may be absent (Fig. 155). Woods that have vestured vessel pits sometimes also have vestured perforation plate openings [22, 84, 116, 117]. Vestures can occur on the borders of the individual openings in both scalariform (Fig. 156) and simple (Fig. 157) perforation plates. Since neither vestures nor a warty layer ever occur on the ridge between the secondary wall borders of perforations, it can be assumed that these features are deposited prior to the removal of the perforation partition.

4.3 Vessel pitting

The side walls of vessel elements are normally interrupted by pits. The density and nature of the pits vary depending on the number and nature of the contiguous cells. Pits connecting one vessel element to another are termed *intervessel pits* and are usually more prolific than those connecting the vessel element with most other cell types (Fig. 158). Intervessel pits are usually bordered with narrow elliptical pit apertures orientated at a large angle to the long axis of the cell.

Intervessel pits may be divided into two broad categories, *scalariform* and *circular*, depending on the outline of the pit membrane. Scalariform pits occur in a ladderlike arrangement (Fig. 160) similar to the individual

Fig. 154. Part of a long scalariform perforation plate in a vessel close to the cambium in *Laurelia novae-zelandiae* A. Cunn. (Atherospermataceae) with microfibrillar webs present in all the perforations. RLF × 1650.

Fig. 155. A simple perforation plate lacking overarching borders in *Aristotelia serrata* (J. R. et G. Forst.) W. R. B. Oliver (Elaeocarpaceae). RLF × 1000.

Fig. 156. Vestured scalariform perforation plate openings in *Neomyrtus pedunculata* (Hook.f.) Allan. RLF × 10 500.

Fig. 157. A vestured simple perforation plate in *Leptospermum ericoides* A. Rich. (Myrtaceae). RLF × 5000.

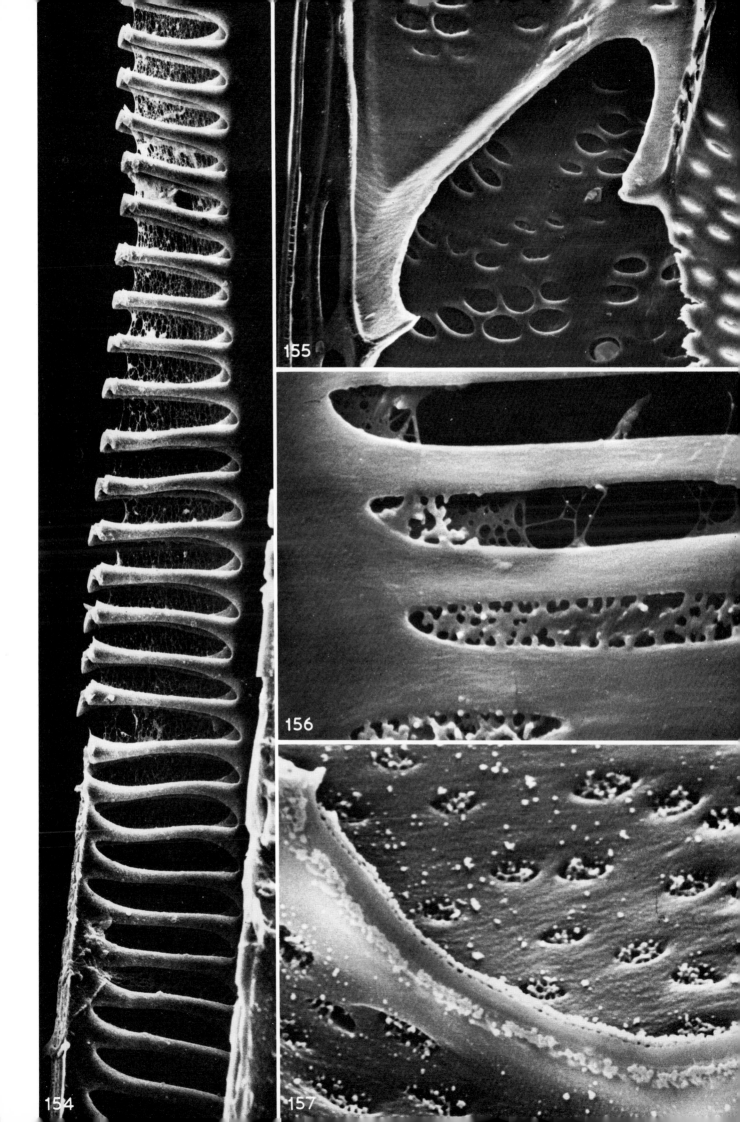

openings in a scalariform perforation plate. Circular pits are usually close packed in an *alternate* (Fig. 159) or less commonly in an *opposite* arrangement [45] (Fig. 161) or more frequently a combination of both. Woods with scalariform perforation plates tend to have scalariform or opposite pitting or both, while woods with simple perforation plates tend to have mostly alternate pitting.

Intervessel pit membranes are usually of uniform thickness and sometimes show a microfibrillar texture under the scanning electron microscope [19] (Fig. 14), though membranes with a distinct torus and margo as in conifer earlywood tracheids have been observed in a few woods [119]. Some degradation of the membranes is usually apparent close to perforation plates, especially the first few scalariform or opposite pits close to the end of a scalariform perforation plate [93, 97, 158] (Figs. 140 and 162).

Intervessel pits are vestured (Figs. 19, 22 – 26, 163 and 164) in some or all of the woods of certain dicotyledonous families [90]. When present, these vestures line the inside of the pit aperture and chamber (Figs. 19 and 163) and sometimes spread out like a warty layer on the lumen surface of the vessel wall [23, 116] (Figs. 22 and 164) (*see* Section 1.2).

Vessel to parenchyma pits are also normally bordered. In some woods they are similar in outline and arrangement to the intervessel pits. In many woods, however, the vessel to axial parenchyma pits, although bordered, have distinctly larger pit apertures than the intervessel pits (Fig. 165). Vessel to ray parenchyma pits may also be larger than the intervessel pits and are frequently grouped into *cross fields* (Fig. 166). Vessel to axial and ray parenchyma pits may be vestured in woods with vestured intervessel pits (Fig. 20), but the vesturing tends to be less dramatic and may be absent from many pits (Fig. 200).

Vessel to fibre pitting is usually very sparse, the walls of vessels contiguous with fibres often showing no pitting at all (Fig. 158). When present, vessel to fibre pits are small, bordered and have narrow, elliptical apertures.

Vessel walls may also be overlaid with helical thickenings. These are described in Section 1.3 and illustrated in Figures 28 – 32 and 34 – 37.

4.4 Vascular and vasicentric tracheids

While water conduction is performed in most hardwoods by perforated vessel elements joined end to end to form a vessel, some hardwoods also have imperforate tracheids present. These cells, which are intermediate in form between fibres and vessel elements, probably assist more with conduction than support.

Vascular tracheids resemble narrow vessel elements but lack perforation plates in their end walls. They are

Fig. 158. The density and nature of the pitting in a vessel depends on the nature of the contiguous cells. In these vessels of *Nothofagus solandri var. solandri* (Hook.f.) Oerst. (Fagaceae), the intervessel pitting is prolific but vessel to fibre pitting is virtually absent. Some vessel to ray pits can be seen in the top left corner of the micrograph. TF × 1200.

Fig. 159. Alternate intervessel pitting in *Salix alba* L. (Salicaceae). TLF × 1550.

Fig. 160. Scalariform intervessel pitting in *Laurelia novae-zelandiae* A. Cunn. (Atherospermataceae). RLF × 1250.

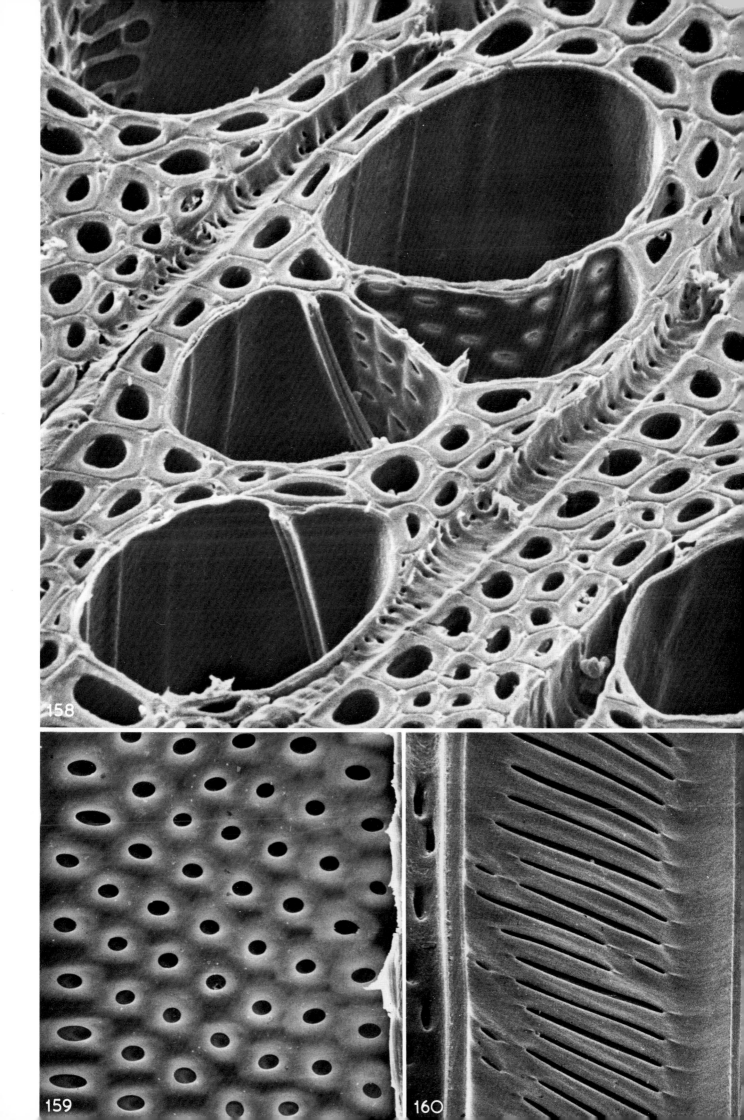

158

159

160

usually arranged in vertical series like small vessels [122]. Their lateral as well as their end walls are usually interrupted with numerous small bordered pits. Helical thickenings may also be present. Vascular tracheids may be degenerate vessel elements where the perforation plate has been lost [27]. They are known to occur in specialized representatives of advanced families and are usually found alongside cells of similar dimensions possessing perforation plates. In transverse sections it is impossible to distinguish between vascular tracheids and vessels. Scanning electron microscope observations of many woods claimed to possess vascular tracheids have shown that small perforations are in fact present in many of the cells often claimed to be vascular tracheids so their occurrence in hardwoods may not be as common as is often claimed.

Vasicentric tracheids are unusual tracheids confined to the Fagaceae and to *Fraxinus* [37]. They resemble vascular tracheids but do not lie in vertical series. They are usually found associated with the vessels and tend to have rounded ends, thin walls and numerous small bordered pits.

Vascular and vasicentric tracheids differ from conifer tracheids in that they do not lie in radial files and their radial and tangential walls are pitted more or less equally by bordered pit-pairs separated by intact pit membranes.

4.5 Fibres

Fibres make up a high proportion of the volume of most hardwoods (Fig. 167). They are imperforate, axially elongated cells, generally of small diameter, that taper at each end to pointed tips. Their secondary walls are usually sparsely pitted and considerably thicker than those of vessel elements and axial and ray parenchyma cells. Normally they have no living contents at maturity. Their primary function is support.

Xylem fibres are usually considerably longer than the cambial fusiform initials from which they are derived [175]. The elongation varies within any one growth ring, between different parts of the tree and between different woods. The importance of fibre length to the pulp and paper industry has led to intense research into this aspect of wood anatomy [44].

Fibre wall thickness also varies; within-ring, within-tree and between species differences all being evident. Five categories are commonly used to classify the average fibre wall thickness based on their appearance in a cut transverse face. These are:

Very thin walled – wall thickness much less than fibre lumen diameter.

Thin walled – wall thickness slightly less than fibre lumen diameter.

Fig. 161. Opposite intervessel pitting in *Nothofagus solandri* var. *cliffortioides* (Hook.f.) Poole (Fagaceae). TLF × 2500.

Fig. 162. Microfibrillar webs traversing the last few openings in a scalariform perforation plate in *Dracophyllum longifolium* (J. F. et G. Forst.) R.Br. (Epacridaceae). RLF × 3750.

Fig. 163. Vestured alternate intervessel pitting in *Eugenia maire* A. Cunn. (Myrtaceae). RLF × 3000.

Fig. 164. Vestured intervessel pitting in *Eucalyptus* sp. (Myrtaceae). In this genus the vestures sometimes occlude the pit aperture and spread out on the vessel wall. RLF × 3250.

Fig. 165. Vessel to axial parenchyma pitting in *Paratrophis microphylla* (Raoul) Ckn. (Moraceae). These pits lie in rows because of the form of the contiguous parenchyma strands. Small, alternate intervessel pits can also be seen in the walls between the vessels. RLF × 750.

Fig. 166. Vessel to ray crossfield pitting in *Nothofagus truncata* (Col.) Ckn. (Fagaceae). Rows of small, opposite intervessel pits can also be seen in the walls between the vessels. RLF × 600.

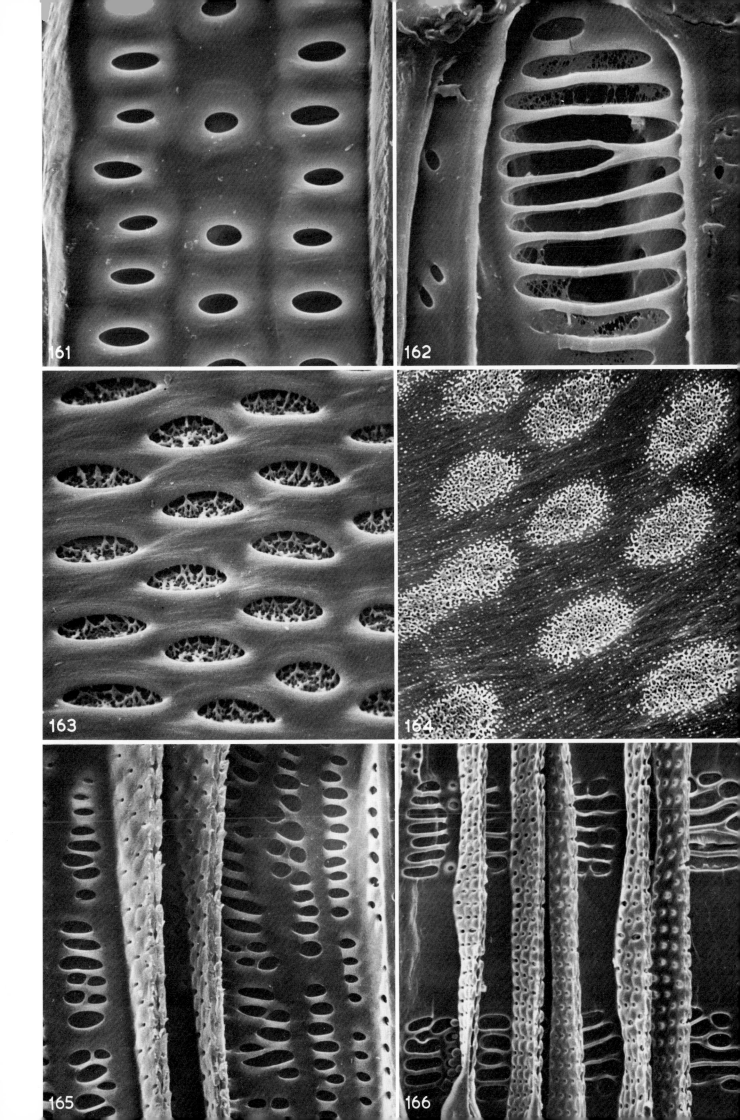

Moderately thick walled – wall thickness about the same as the fibre lumen diameter.

Thick walled – wall thickness greater than the fibre lumen diameter.

Very thick walled – wall so thick that the fibre lumen is almost closed up.

In a cut transverse face, fibres commonly show considerable variation in both overall diameter and cell wall thickness. This effect results from the tapering outline of the cells. The fibres visible in any one cross-section will include some that have been cut near the midpoint of their length where they are widest, and some that have been cut near their tip where their transverse dimensions are small and their lumina apparently almost non-existent (Fig. 168). Since the tapering ends of the cells occupy less of the total length of the fibre than does the central region of uniform diameter, small thick walled fibres appear to be less abundant in a cut transverse section than do the larger ones. Fibres are sometimes radially compressed in the latewood similar to the latewood tracheids of conifers (Fig. 169).

The proportion of fibres present and the average thickness of their cell walls, largely govern the density of a hardwood. Very dense woods have a high proportion of fibres present and these have thick to very thick walls. Very light woods have a lower proportion of fibres and these have thin walls. Woods of intermediate density have various combinations of these factors.

Fibres are usually subdivided into libriform fibres and fibre tracheids depending on their length, wall thickness and the nature of their pits. *Libriform fibres* are longer than fibre-tracheids. They have moderately thick to very thick walls with simple pits (Figs. 16, 170 and 172). Their function is primarily one of support. *Fibre-tracheids* are not usually as long as libriform fibres. They have thin to moderately thick walls with bordered pits (Fig. 11, 169, and 171). They function both in conduction and support though their occurrence in porous woods suggest that support is their prime function. It is likely that they represent an intermediate evolutionary form between the tracheid and the libriform fibre.

Many hardwoods, belonging to several dicotyledonous families have libriform fibres and fibre tracheids that are subdivided into a number of chambers by thin transverse walls across their lumina [25, 48, 179] (Figs. 173 and 174). Such fibres are termed *septate fibres* and the thin cross walls *septa*. The septa develop after normal secondary wall deposition has ended following late division of the fibre cytoplasm and renewed cell wall formation [123, 178]. Where a septum meets the secondary wall of the fibre it separates into two thinner layers each spreading out on the lumen surface of the secondary wall (Fig. 175). These new walls are easily separated from the secondary wall of the fibre [25] (Figs. 175 and 176) but otherwise have many of the

Fig. 167. Transverse face of the wood of *Sophora tetraptera* J. Mill. (Papilionaceae). Over 50 per cent of the wood volume is built up of thick walled libriform fibres, with the vessels and axial parenchyma cells grouped into irregular clusters. TF × 60.

Fig. 168. Thin walled fibres in *Tectona grandis* L.f. (Verbenaceae). The fibres show considerable variation in diameter. This is because some have been cut almost in half at their widest point, while others have been cut near their tips where their transverse dimensions are small and their lumina constricted. TF × 600.

Fig. 169. Radially compressed latewood fibre tracheids in the wood of *Quercus coccinea* Muench. (Fagaceae). Note the bordered pits in the radial and tangential walls ,in both the latewood and the earlywood cells. TF × 1250.

Fig. 170. Very thick walled libriform fibres in *Hoheria angustifolia* Raoul (Malvaceae). The lumina in the fibres of this wood are almost non-existent. The larger cell to the lower right is an axial parenchyma cell while that to the upper right is part of a ray parenchyma cell. The cutting lines are an artifact of specimen preparation. TF × 3250.

Fig. 171. Bordered pits with lenticular inner apertures in fibre tracheids of *Dracophyllum traversii* Hook.f. (Epacridaceae). The pit apertures approximately follow the angle of the S_2 microfibrils. RLF × 4000.

Fig. 172. Thick walled libriform fibres with narrow slit-extended pit apertures in *Beilschmiedia tawa* (A. Cunn.) Benth. (Lauraceae). Note the 'brooming' of the left hand wall of each fibre. This preparation artifact is due to the razor blade cutting 'against the grain' of the S_2 layer microfibrils in the left hand walls, but 'with the grain' of the microfibrils in the right hand walls. RLF × 2100.

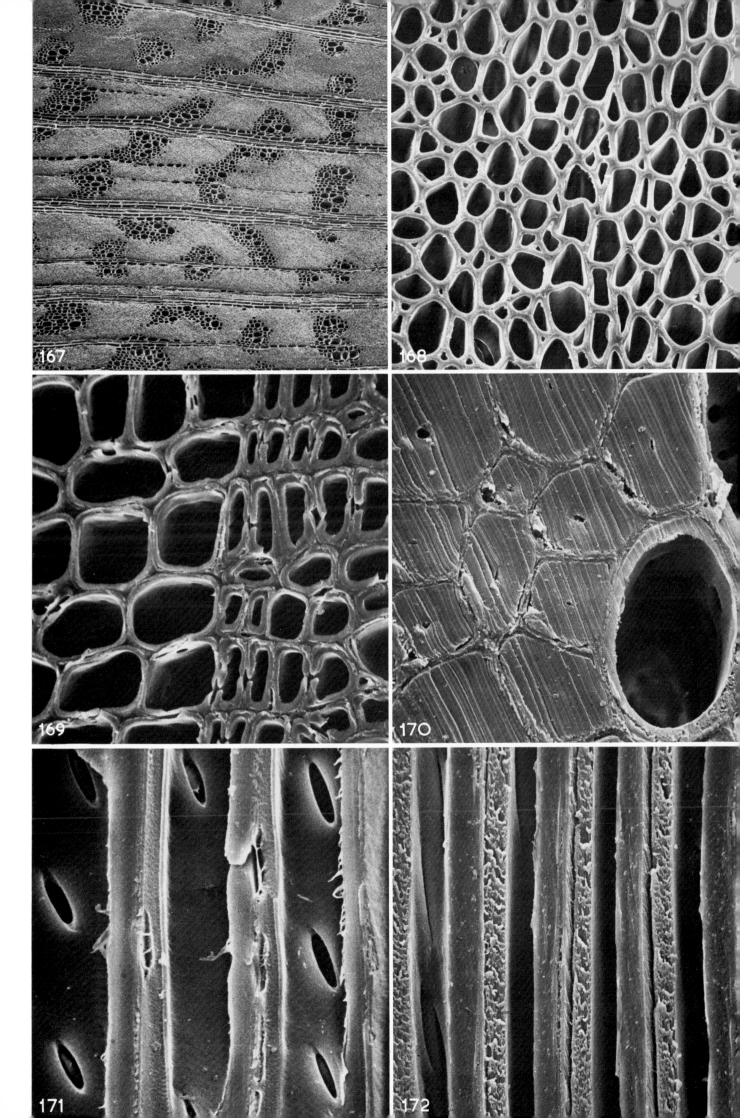

167

168

169

170

171

172

characteristics of a normal primary wall layer. Where stretched, the septum separates into microfibrillar webs [25] (Fig. 176). The new wall layer does not usually obstruct pit apertures but occasionally it overlies the inner aperture of pits close to the septum [25] (Fig. 176) and more rarely the septum itself traverses the cell lumen at a point opposite a pit (Fig. 177) thereby occluding the entrance to the pit canal.

Septate fibres in most hardwoods function as the site for the deposition of various storage products including starches (Fig. 173), oils and resins. Their abundance in woods with sparse axial parenchyma has led to the suggestion that they have evolved to provide an alternative storage site for such materials. They are not always seen in macerated wood preparations as the septa are easily removed by most macerating agents.

Fibres in the tension wood of certain hardwoods are modified to form tension wood fibres (Figs. 223 – 226). These fibres differ from normal libriform fibres and fibre tracheids in having an inner wall layer, the *gelatinous layer*, that differs both in its chemical composition and in its physical properties from the normal secondary wall layers. Tension wood fibres are described more fully in Section 4.12.

The lumen surfaces of fibre walls are usually smooth and interrupted only by the pit apertures, though helical thickenings do occur in the fibres of a few hardwoods (Fig. 178). A fine warty layer is sometimes present and in some woods where the fibre pits are vestured, vestures may spread out on the lumen surface of the fibre wall [23, 100] (Fig. 27).

Fibre pits may be simple or bordered (*see* Section 1.2) depending on the nature of the fibre and are usually more numerous on the radial walls. Generally fibre pitting is sparse compared with that in many other cell walls. The pit membranes are small and generally circular in outline. The length of the pit canal depends on the thickness of the fibre wall, but its diameter is often very small and partially obstructed by a network of microfibrils (Fig. 16). The inner pit apertures are usually extended with the lenticular to slit-shaped opening following the general orientation of the S_2 microfibrils (Figs. 12, 21, 171 and 172).

4.6 Axial parenchyma

Axial parenchyma (also called *longitudinal* or *vertical* parenchyma) is generally more abundant in hardwoods than in softwoods. Like the vessel elements and fibres, axial parenchyma is derived from the fusiform initials of the vascular cambium. However, unlike vessel elements and fibres where each derivative of the cambium becomes one vessel element or one fibre, a number of axial parenchyma cells usually develop end to end by segmentation from each cambial fusiform cell to form a *strand*

Fig. 173. Septate fibres in a radial longitudinal face of *Fuchsia excorticata* (J. R. et G. Forst.) Linn. f. (Onagraceae). The spherical bodies are starch grains. RLF × 1650.

Fig. 174. A septate fibre seen in a transverse face of *Fuchsia excorticata*. TF × 4600.

Fig. 175. Detail of a fibre septum in *Griselinia lucida* Forst.f. (Griseliniaceae). The septum has partly separated from the fibre wall revealing its two layered nature and its relationship to the fibre secondary wall. RLF × 4000.

Fig. 176. A fibre septum that has partly separated from the secondary wall and formed a microfibrillar web in *Gaultheria antipoda* Forst.f. (Ericaceae). The septum layer occasionally obstructs the apertures of pits. RLF × 7250.

Fig. 177. A fibre septum that has formed over the top of a pit aperture in *Myrsine divaricata* A. Cunn. (Myrsinaceae). RLF × 4200.

Fig. 178. Fibre-tracheids with helical thickenings in *Pennantia corymbosa* J. R. et G. Forst. (Icacinaceae). RLF × 2200.

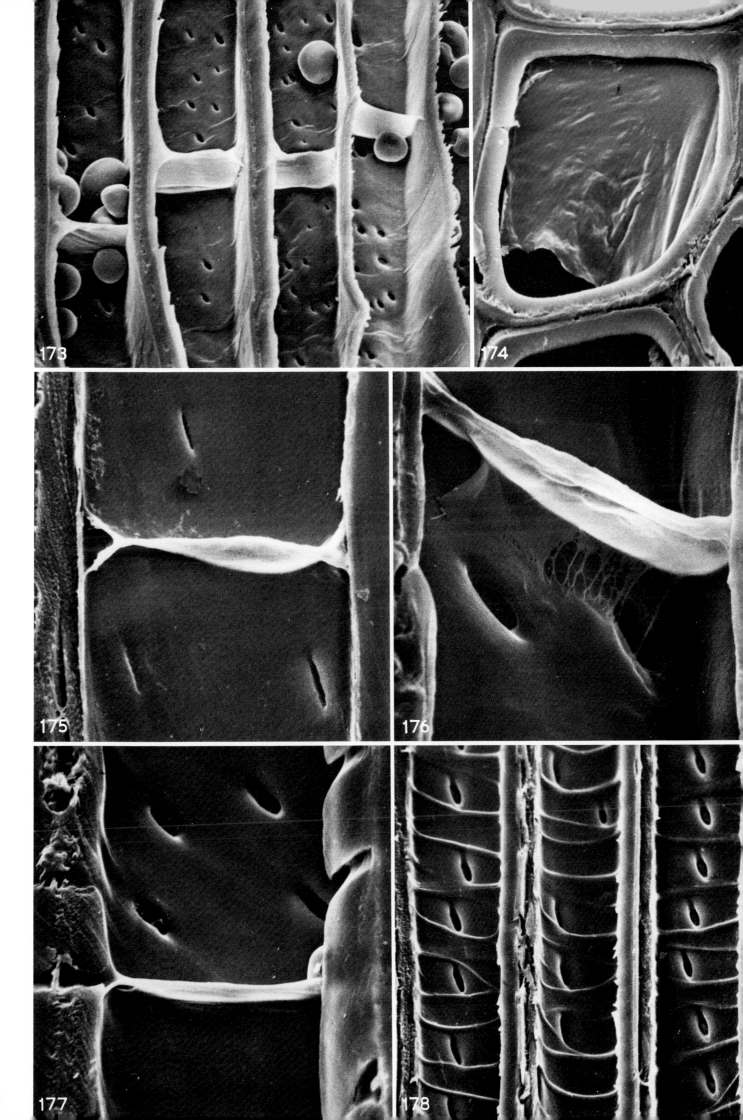

(Fig. 179). Strands are commonly made up of two, four, eight or more cells joined end to end. Most of the cells in a strand have transverse end walls but the cells at each end of a strand may have pointed tips.

The distribution of the axial parenchyma within the growth ring is usually diagnostic for a particular wood and may be of value in its identification. Three broad categories are defined: *paratracheal* axial parenchyma is always associated with vessels and vascular tracheids (Fig. 180), *apotracheal* axial parenchyma does not have any relationship (Figs. 181 – 183), while *boundary* parenchyma always lies at the end or beginning of a growth ring (Fig. 184).

Paratracheal parenchyma may consist of the occasional isolated strand or strands associated with a vessel, but never ensheathing it, termed *scanty paratracheal* parenchyma (Fig. 181) or parenchyma strands may completely ensheath the vessel forming *vasicentric paratracheal* parenchyma (Fig. 180). Vasicentric paratracheal parenchyma expanded into tangential wings on either side of the vessel or vessel groups is described as *aliform* parenchyma while the linking of such groups of parenchyma forms *aliform confluent* parenchyma.

Apotracheal parenchyma may be distributed as isolated strands of cells amidst the fibres, giving the appearance in transverse section of being isolated single cells (Fig. 181) or it may be distributed in small groups of strands usually in tangential rows (Fig. 182). The former type is described as *diffuse* axial parenchyma while the latter as *diffuse-in-aggregates*. More extensive bands of apotracheal parenchyma, alternating with the fibres, occur in some hardwoods and here the distribution is said to be *banded apotracheal* (Figs. 138, 183 and 204).

Boundary parenchyma is usually described as either *terminal* or *initial* (Fig. 184) depending on whether or not it lies at the end of one growth ring or the beginning of the next. Terminal and initial axial parenchyma are often difficult to separate even at the electron microscope level and may simply be referred to as *boundary* or *marginal* parenchyma.

Many woods have more than one type of axial parenchyma present and distributions intermediate between these main categories can occur.

Axial parenchyma cells are usually characterized by having thinnish secondary walls interrupted by small circular simple pits irregularly disposed (Figs. 185 and 186). The walls are never as thick as those of libriform fibres (Fig. 180) but may in some woods approximate the thickness of the walls of fibre tracheids and vessels. Instances of helical thickenings in axial parenchyma cells have been recorded in some woods [173] (Fig. 187).

The protoplast within each axial parenchyma cell is long lived and responsible for tylose development in some woods (*see* Section 4.9). Its death is usually associated with heartwood formation. Axial parenchyma

Fig. 179. Axial parenchyma cells in *Corynocarpus laevigatus* J. R. et G. Forst (Corynocarpaceae). Axial parenchyma cells normally lie in vertical strands, each strand being derived from a fusiform cambial cell by segmentation. A comparison of the lengths of the axial parenchyma cells and the vessel elements show that most strands consist of two axial parenchyma cells in this particular wood. RLF × 200.

Fig. 180. Vasicentric paratracheal axial parenchyma surrounding four vessels in *Dodonaea viscosa* Jacquin (Sapindaceae). TF × 350.

Fig. 181. Diffuse (D) and diffuse-in-aggregates (DA) apotracheal and scanty vascientric (V) axial parenchyma in *Fagus sylvatica* L. (Fagaceae). TF × 700.

Fig. 182. Diffuse-in-aggregates apotracheal axial parenchyma in *Melicope ternata* J. R. et G. Forst. (Rutaceae). TF × 400.

Fig. 183. Banded apotracheal axial parenchyma in *Paratrophis microphylla* (Raoul) Ckn. (Moraceae) TF × 80.

Fig. 184. Growth ring boundaries (arrowed) demarcated by bands of initial boundary axial parenchyma in the earlywood of *Nestegis lanceolata* (Hook.f.) L. Johnson (Oleaceae). TF × 100.

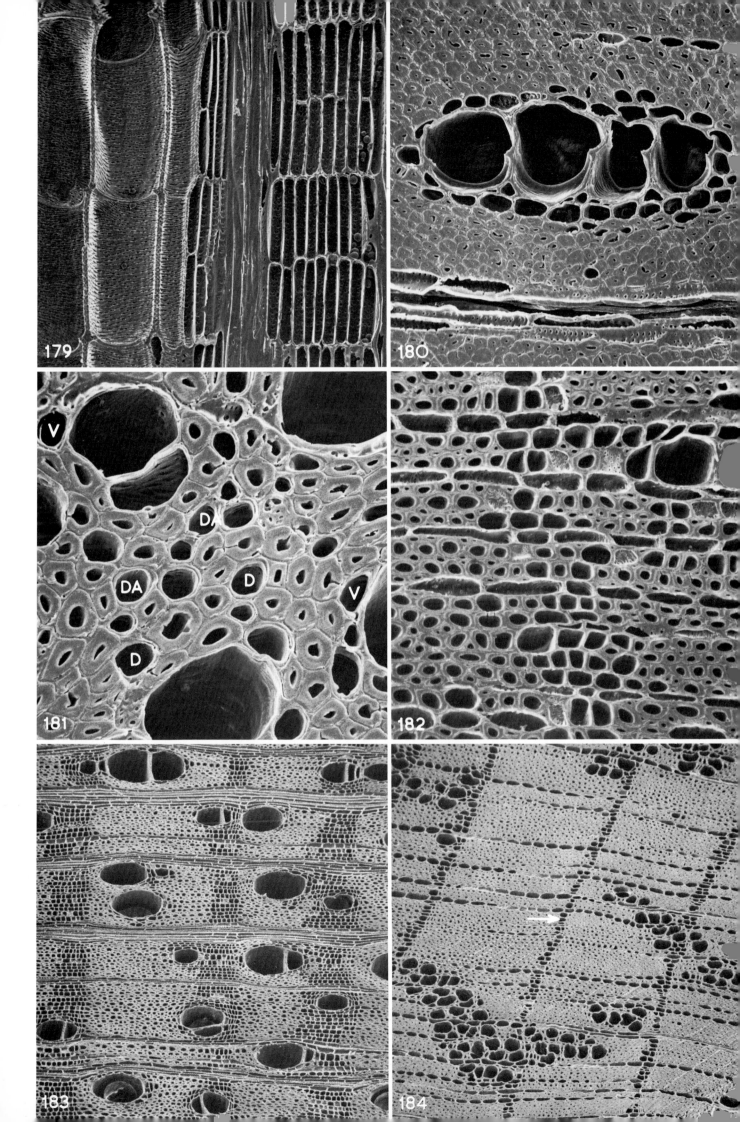

may contain starch grains, raphides or other crystals, and other inclusions (*see* Section 1.5) in which case the cells may be chambered (Fig. 188).

Unusual forms of parenchyma that are more iso-diametric or cubical than axial, are found in a number of woods. Some members of the Tiliaceae, for example, have broad concentric bands of thin walled, irregular shaped parenchyma cells alternating with the other axial cell types (Figs. 189 and 190). This pattern develops in certain other woods from the action of successive cambia. In such cases normal longitudinal axial paren-chyma may develop in the wood produced endarch to each cambium, while isodiametric parenchyma, phloem and sclereids may be produced in the exarch position. The development of successive cambia leaves the wood with the appearance of concentric bands of thin walled parenchyma.

4.7 Rays

The rays in hardwood are generally larger and more variable in size than those found in softwoods (*cf.* Figs. 53 and 54 with 130 and 131). Softwood rays are almost entirely uniseriate with a tendency to part or wholly biseriate in some woods. True multiseriate rays are very rare and usually associated with radial resin canals. Hardwoods, on the other hand, commonly possess broad multiseriate rays (Figs. 191, 192 and 194) though there is a high degree of variability. A few hardwoods, such as the willows, possess only uniseriate rays (Figs. 193 and 201). Some hardwoods have rays of two distinct sizes – short uniseriates, and broad, high multiseriates (Fig. 194), while others have an almost complete range of ray sizes. Many wood antomical descriptions put much emphasis on the range of possible ray widths. While the maximum ray width and the proportion of uniseriates to multiseriates may be significant, in practice ray width may be so variable as to render the character almost useless in wood identification. Since ray height tends to be related to ray width (as seen in the tangential plane), a similar variability in ray height can be expected in most hardwoods.

Many large rays in certain hardwoods are really only clusters of smaller rays, each separated by a few axial elements (Fig. 195). Such rays are termed *aggregate rays* and result from uneven circumferential growth of the cambium. It is not always easy to distinguish between aggregate rays and *dissected rays*. The latter rays, while giving the appearance of aggregate rays, result from the splitting of a ray by the intrusive growth of fusiform initials between the ray initials in the cambial zone.

An explanation as to why ray height and width vary so enormously is only possible from an understanding of the processes occurring in the vascular cambium with secondary growth. As the vascular cambium lays down

Fig. 185. A strand of axial parenchyma cells lying between fibre-tracheids of similar wall thickness in *Carpinus betulinus* L. (Carponaceae). Note the branched pits. RLF × 2900.

Fig. 186. Simple pit-pairs connecting contiguous axial parenchyma cells in *Archeria traversii* Hook.f. (Epacrida-ceae). RLF × 2000.

Fig. 187. Helical thickenings on the wall of an axial parenchyma cell in *Cyathodes fasciculata* (Forst.f.) Allan (Epacridaceae). RLF × 1250.

Fig. 188. Chambered axial parenchyma cells in *Cyathodes fasciculata*. These strands develop by the repeated division of fusiform cambial cells to produce axial files of small cells. They usually contain crystals – *see* Fig. 43. RLF × 375.

Fig. 189. A band of thin walled angular axial parenchyma cells in *Entelea arborescens* R.Br. (Tiliaceae). These bands alternate with vessels, fibres and longitudinal axial parenchyma cells. TF × 250.

Fig. 190. Detail of thin walled angular axial paren-chyma cells in *Entelea arborescens*. TF/RLF × 600.

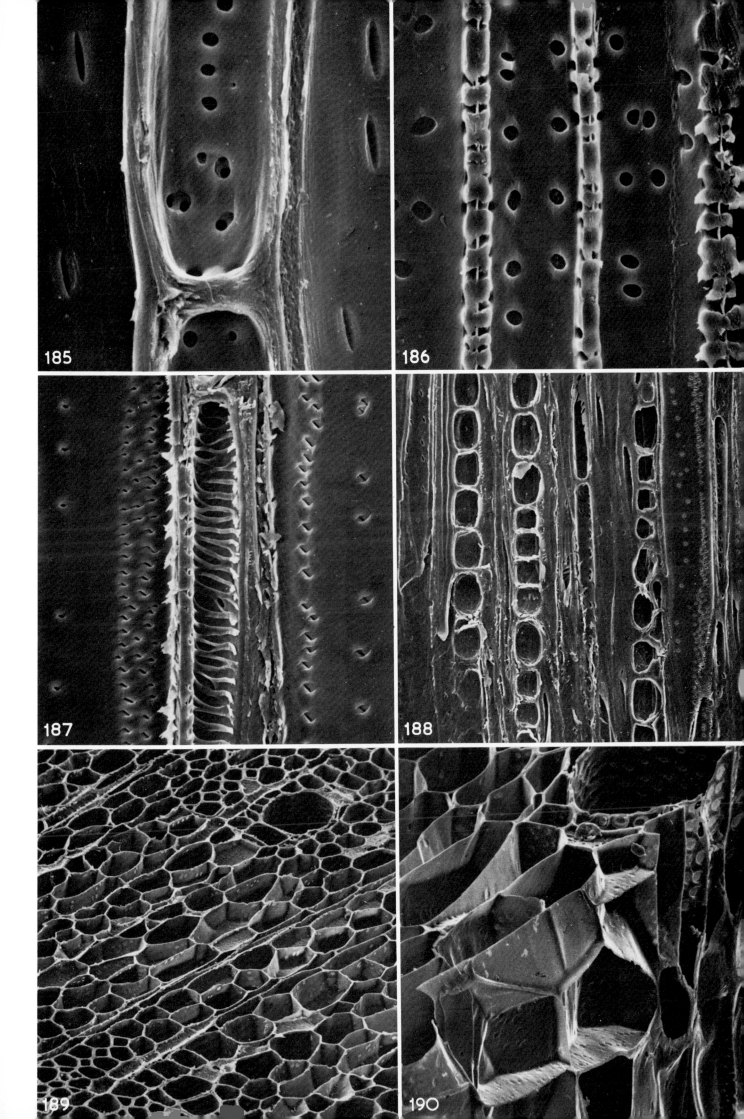

185

186

187

188

189

190

new wood, the cambial circumference increases. As most woods maintain a constant ratio of axial to ray elements, new rays must be constantly added to the cambial cylinder as radial growth proceeds. New rays arise in the cambium and enter a cycle of development in which they increase in size and split into smaller units which may increase in size again. As these processes are occurring simultaneously with radial growth, the resulting size changes are reflected in the size of the differentiated rays in the wood.

Hardwood rays are composed almost exclusively of parenchyma cells. The occurrence of ray tracheids and vessels is rare [165]. Parenchyma cells can be of a number of shapes and the proportions of the various cell shapes is usually characteristic for a particular wood. The most common shape for a ray parenchyma cell is a blunt ended cylinder, radially elongated in the stem. Such cells are termed *procumbent* cells (Fig. 196). The second most common shape for ray parenchyma cells in hardwoods is a more or less rectangular cell with its long axis aligned along the vertical axis of the stem. Such cells are termed *upright* cells. Rays built up entirely of either procumbent or upright cells are termed *homogenous* or *homocellular* rays. Homogenous rays may be uniseriate or multiseriate. Both procumbent and upright cells, however, are usually found in association with one another in the same ray (Fig. 197). The upright cells tend to form uniseriate extensions or fins at the upper and lower extremities of the ray (Figs. 192 and 198), though sometimes the upright cells completely surround the procumbent core of the ray. Upright cells on the lateral extremities of the ray are termed *sheath cells* (Fig. 199). Rays containing both procumbent and upright cells are termed *heterogenous* or *heterocellular* rays. Heterogenous rays may be uniseriate or multiseriate. It has sometimes been found helpful to indicate the proportions of upright to procumbent parenchyma cells by subdividing the rays into three categories:

Heterogenous Type I – uniseriates composed of upright or upright and procumbent cells; the multiseriates having uniseriate tails of upright cells longer than the multiseriate part.

Heterogenous Type II – uniseriates composed of upright or upright and procumbent cells; the multiseriates having uniseriate tails shorter than the multiseriate part and composed of upright and procumbent cells or a single marginal row of upright cells.

Heterogenous Type III – uniseriates composed of upright, or upright and procumbent cells; the multiseriates having uniseriate tails composed of only one row of upright cells.

A third form of parenchyma cell occurs in the rays of some hardwoods. These cells are often almost cubical in shape and are termed *tile* cells because of the regular pattern of squares they present when seen in a transverse

Fig. 191. Broad multiseriate rays 5 – 25 or more cells wide in *Schefflera digitata* J. R. et G. Forst. (Araliaceae). TLF × 40.

Fig. 192. Multiseriate rays, 2 – 8 cells wide, heterogenous type II in *Beilschmiedia tawa* (A. Cunn.) Benth. et Hook.f. ex Kirk (Lauraceae). TLF × 100.

Fig. 193. Uniseriate, homogeneous rays in *Aesculus hippocastanum* L. (Hippocastanaceae). TLF × 300.

Fig. 194. Some woods contain rays of two sizes, high broad multiseriate and short narrow uniseriates or biseriates as in *Quercus robur* Liebl. (Fagaceae). TF/TLF × 160.

Fig. 195. An aggregate ray built up of a cluster of small uniseriate rays in *Alnus glutinosa* Gaertn. (Betulaceae). TF/TLF × 190.

Fig. 196. Procumbent ray parenchyma cells in *Knightia excelsa* R.Br. (Proteaceae). TLF/RLF × 320.

Fig. 197. Upright (U) and procumbent (P) ray parenchyma in a heterogenous ray of *Fagus sylvatica* L. (Fagaceae). TLF/RLF × 800.

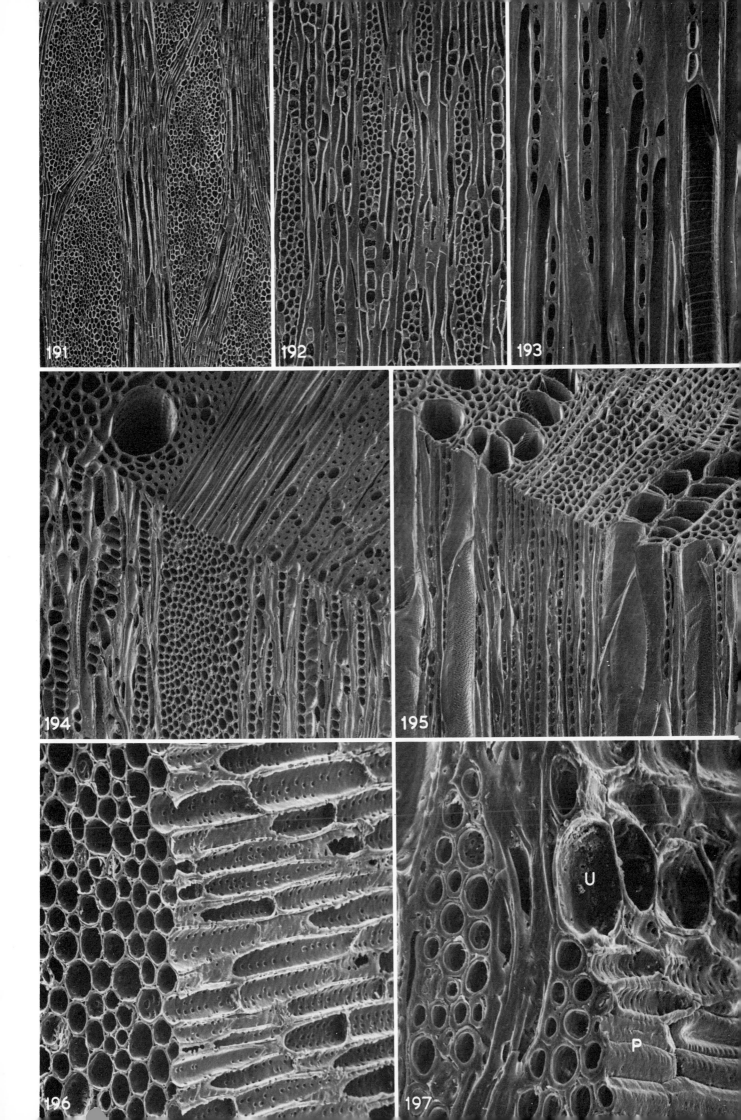

cut through a ray. Upright tile cells have been described as being present in a number of woods, but it is often difficult to distinguish them from normal upright parenchyma cells occurring in the main body of the multiseriate ray. Rays with such mixed procumbent and upright cells throughout are sometimes termed *heterogenous irregular* rays.

The walls of the ray parenchyma cells are usually secondarily thickened and generally similar in thickness to those of the axial parenchyma cells (Fig. 196). The end walls are either vertical or oblique. Pitting is usually fairly prolific on the radial walls (Fig. 196) especially when the pits form pit-pairs with contiguous vessel elements or tracheids. Ray to vessel pits may occur between any ray cell and the contiguous vessel (Fig. 200), or they may link only the upright cells at the extremities of the ray with the vessel (Figs. 166 and 201). Such ray cells are termed *contact* cells. Pit-pairs connecting ray parenchyma to fibres tend to be sparse. Pits also occur on the end and tangential walls of most cells thereby connecting contiguous ray parenchyma cells. The pits are exclusively simple, usually small and circular but sometimes oval or scalariform. Intercellular spaces are common and are often connected to the ray parenchyma cells by blind pits.

The protoplast within each ray parenchyma cell is long lived and along with those of the axial parenchyma cells is responsible for tylose development in some woods (*see* Section 4.9). The death of the ray cell protoplast is usually associated with heartwood formation.

Hardwood ray parenchyma cells, like those of the axial parenchyma, frequently contain various sorts of inclusions such as crystals, gums and amorphous substances (*see* Section 1.5).

It is often claimed that living parenchyma cells are essential for the functioning of the vertical conducting elements of the wood and that a suitable ratio in both amount and distribution between the ray and axial systems must be maintained. While this may be generally true, it does not explain how some woods completely without rays, such as *Hebe* (Scrophulariaceae), can function perfectly well.

4.8 Gums and gum ducts

Organic complexes known as *gums* occur in the vessel elements, fibres and parenchyma cells of certain hardwoods. They may also be deposited in intercellular canals or ducts, and sometimes form in the larger openings in wood known as splits and shakes. Gums are typically viscous white or yellow coloured fluids that ooze out of the wood on sawing.

Gum ducts occur only rarely as a normal feature, being more commonly produced as a result of damage to the cambium resulting from abrasion, insect attack or fire.

Fig. 198. Heterogeneous types I and II rays in *Nestegis lanceolata* (Hook.f.) L. Johnson. TLF × 200.

Fig. 199. Upright cells sometimes ensheath the procumbent ray cells as in *Plagianthus betulinus* A. Cunn. (Malvaceae). Sheath cells indicated (S). TLF × 650.

Fig. 200. Vessel to ray crossfield pitting in *Metrosideros excelsa* Sol. ex Gaertn. (Myrtaceae). In this wood the vessel to procumbent cell pits are vestured while the vessel to upright cell pits generally are not. Oblique TLF × 775.

Fig. 201. In some woods the vessel to ray crossfield pitting is restricted to contact cells at the extremities of the ray, seen here in *Salix alba* L. (Salicaceae). Oblique TLF × 575.

Fig. 202. A transverse gum duct in a multiseriate ray of *Pittosporum tenuifolium* Sol. ex Gaertn. TLF × 450.

Fig. 203. A gum filled duct in *Dodonaea viscosa* Jaquin (Sapindaceae). TLF × 100.

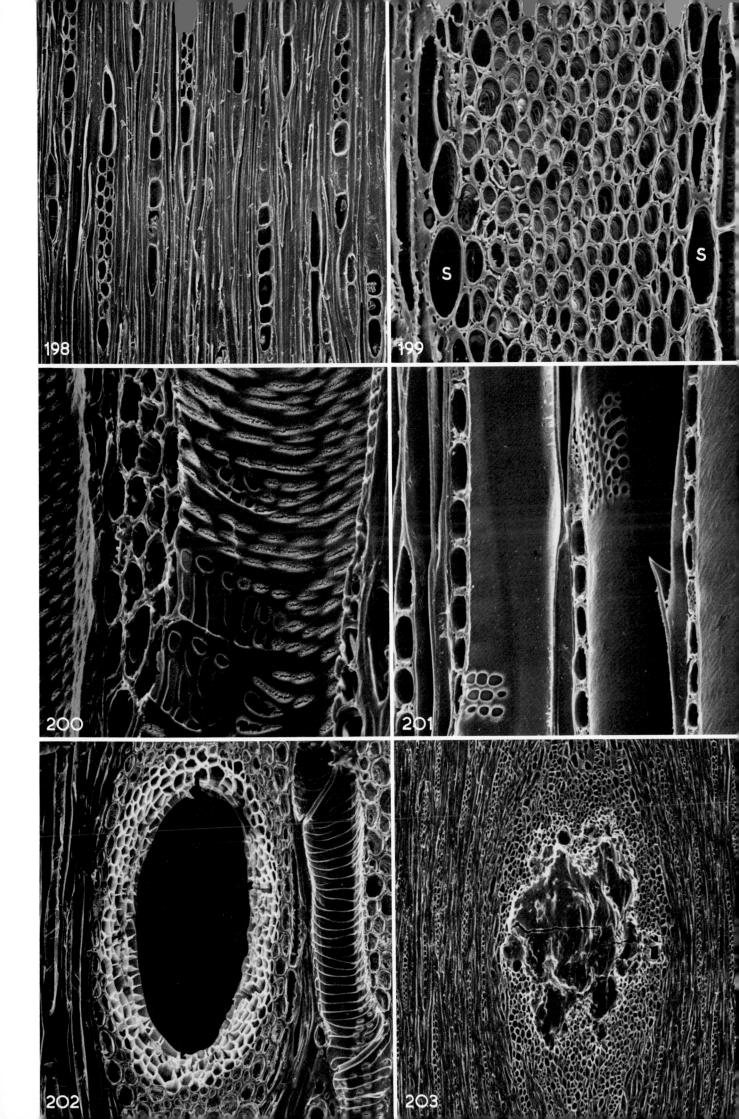

Normal gum ducts occur in almost all the members of the Dipterocarpaceae and in some members of certain other families [90]. Traumatic gum ducts, produced as a result of injury, also tend to develop more commonly in the woods of certain families. They can usually be distinguished from normal ducts because they almost invariably develop in a tangential series and contain dark-coloured, very viscous gums. During initiation, the derivatives of the damaged cambium differentiate into anomalous parenchyma cells. The development of traumatic gum ducts between these cells is similar to that of resin canals in softwoods. In some woods, traumatic ducts may be of such common occurrence that they can be considered a characteristic feature.

Gum ducts may occur in the wood either as axial canals or as transverse canals in the rays (Figs. 202 and 203). More rarely both axial and transverse gum ducts occur in the same wood. Axial gum ducts may occur in tangential groups near the ring boundary, or they may be scattered singly or in small multiples throughout the growth ring. Anastomising gum ducts are known as *gum veins* or *kino veins* and are a traumatic feature of many *Eucalyptus* woods [63].

Intracellular gums may line the walls of vessel elements (Fig. 51) fibres and parenchyma cells (*see* Section 1.5).

4.9 Tyloses

Tyloses are found as normal structures in many hardwoods (Fig. 204). They are outgrowths from axial and ray parenchyma cells [54, 145] that have penetrated through the pits and ballooned out into the lumina of neighbouring cells. They are found most commonly in heartwood vessels though they also occur in sapwood vessels at sites of injury and more rarely in undamaged sapwood. They also occur occasionally in the lumina of fibre-tracheids [55, 139] and in resin canals [5]. They seem to develop only in cells where the pits exceed about 10 microns in diameter.

When numerous tyloses develop from many neighbouring parenchyma cells, the entire vessel can become filled with closely packed tyloses (Fig. 205). Their shape varies considerably depending on how close they are packed. Sometimes they are almost spherical (Fig. 206), while at others they are angular in shape (Fig. 205). Their walls often show thin areas very like primary pit fields (Fig. 207).

Prior to the degradation of the perforation plate partition, the cell walls of axial paratracheal and ray parenchyma cells often become modified by the deposition of a *protective layer* [32, 92, 106, 107, 181]. This layer resembles the primary wall, but is laid down on the lumen side of the normal secondary wall. Deposition occurs towards the end of cell differentiation and apparently seals off the parenchyma cell from the

Fig. 204. Tyloses blocking the vessels in *Paratrophis microphylla* (Raoul) Ckn. (Moraceae). Note also the banded axial parenchyma. TF/TLF × 100.

Fig. 205. Tangential longitudinal view of a vessel in *Paratrophis microphylla* blocked with numerous close packed thin walled tyloses. TLF × 300.

Fig. 206. Spherical tyloses in a vessel of *Paratrophis microphylla*. TLF × 700.

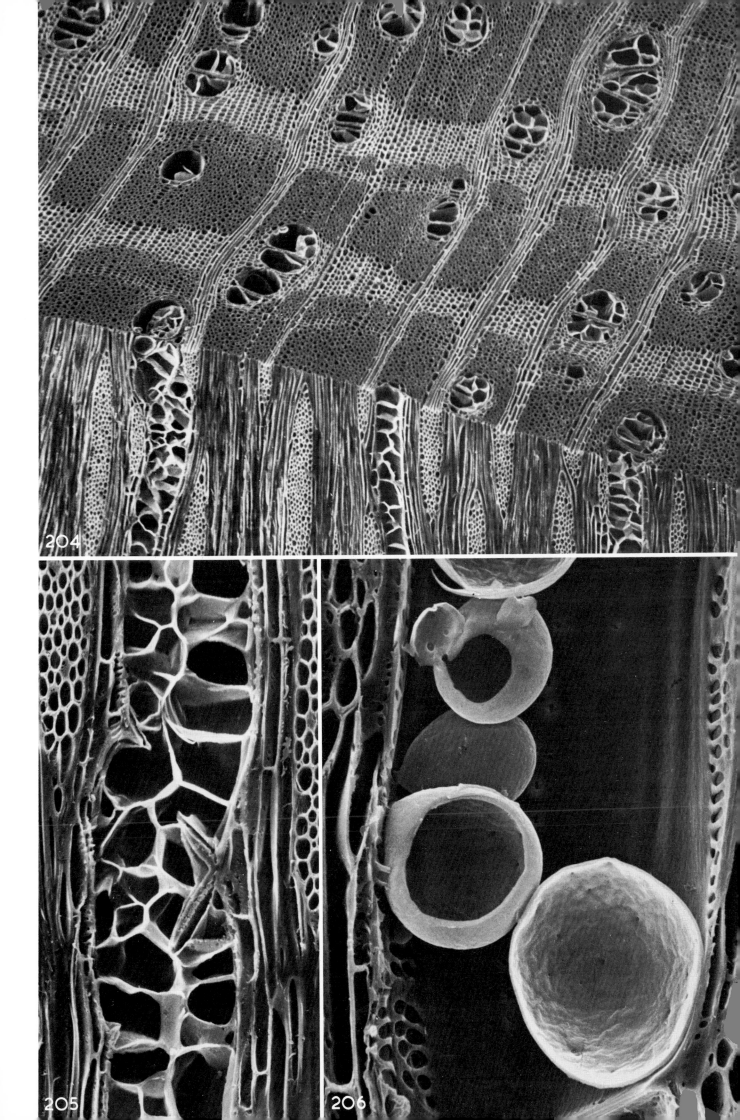

vessel element. The protective layer is laid down over the entire lumen surface of the wall including the pits, but is usually thicker on the walls adjacent to the vessel element (Fig. 208). When the vessel perforation plate partition is enzymatically removed, some pit membranes are apparently also partly or completely degraded. The unlignified protective layer traversing an opened pit aperture then undergoes surface growth and develops into a tylose bud [51, 91, 92, 106] (Fig. 209). These buds have a two layered wall structure [106] and usually balloon out into the vessel lumen until they are stopped by the vessel wall or other tyloses originating from the same or other parenchyma cells. The tylose wall is therefore continuous with the protective layer (Fig. 208). The nucleus and part of the cytoplasm of the parenchyma cell usually pass out into the tylose.

After invading the vessel, the tylose walls may become thickened by the deposition of a multi-layered secondary wall [51, 106] (Fig. 212) and even differentiate into sclereid-like structures filling the vessel with hard walled stone-cells. Tylose secondary walls are often pitted [106, 145], the pits of adjacent tyloses sometimes forming matching pit-pairs.

Tyloses blocking the lumina of vessels reduce the permeability of wood. While this may be advantageous to the tree in isolating sections of damaged wood, it makes the impregnation of such timber by preservatives difficult. Tylose blocked wood, however (e.g. some *Quercus* species), has been traditionally used advantageously in the manufacture of wine casks.

Fungal hyphae can cause abnormal growth of tyloses probably by the release of toxic substances, enzymes or hormones. This may lead ultimately to the death of the tree and is a suggested mechanism of vascular wilt disease [76].

4.10 Included phloem

In some hardwoods, strands of phloem termed *included phloem* [15], may be found embedded within the wood (Figs. 213 – 217). These strands develop in a number of different ways as the result of unusual forms of cambial activity. Their occurrence is confined to some or all of the members of a few angiosperm families and when present can provide a positive character in wood identification.

Included phloem is generally subdivided into two types depending on the distribution of the strands when viewed in the transverse plane. *Foraminate* included phloem strands are scattered more or less randomly throughout the wood while *concentric* included phloem strands, as the term implies, lie in definite rings. Foraminate strands of included phloem develop in one of two ways [141]: in some species the internal derivatives of small arcs of the cambium may, for a short time,

Fig. 207. A spherical tylose blocking a vessel in *Hedycaria arborea* J. R. et G. Forst. (Monimiaceae). Note the primary pit fields. TF × 1500.

Fig. 208. View of a parenchyma cell showing the protective layer (PL) covering the cell wall and pit membranes on the vessel side of the parenchyma cell (P). The protective layer is not present on the opposite side of this cell. Note also how the protective layer passes through the opened pit-pair and into the vessel where it forms the tylose wall (TW). From the wood of *Metrosideros fulgens* Sol. ex Gaertn. (Myrtaceae). TF × 3200.

Fig. 209. Tylose 'buds' growing through vessel wall pits in *Quercus robur* Liebl. (Fagaceae). TLF × 1200.

Fig. 210. A tylose 'ballooning' out into a vessel from a neighbouring parenchyma cell in *Nothofagus solandri* var. *solandri* (Hook.f.) Oerst. (Fagaceae). TF × 1100.

Fig. 211. A fully developed tylose in a vessel of *Nothofagus solandri* var. *solandri* (Fagaceae). The tylose can be seen emerging through an opened pit-pair (arrowed). TF × 1250.

Fig. 212. Detail of the walls of three contiguous tyloses in a vessel of *Quercus robur* showing the multi-layered tylose secondary walls. RLF × 5000.

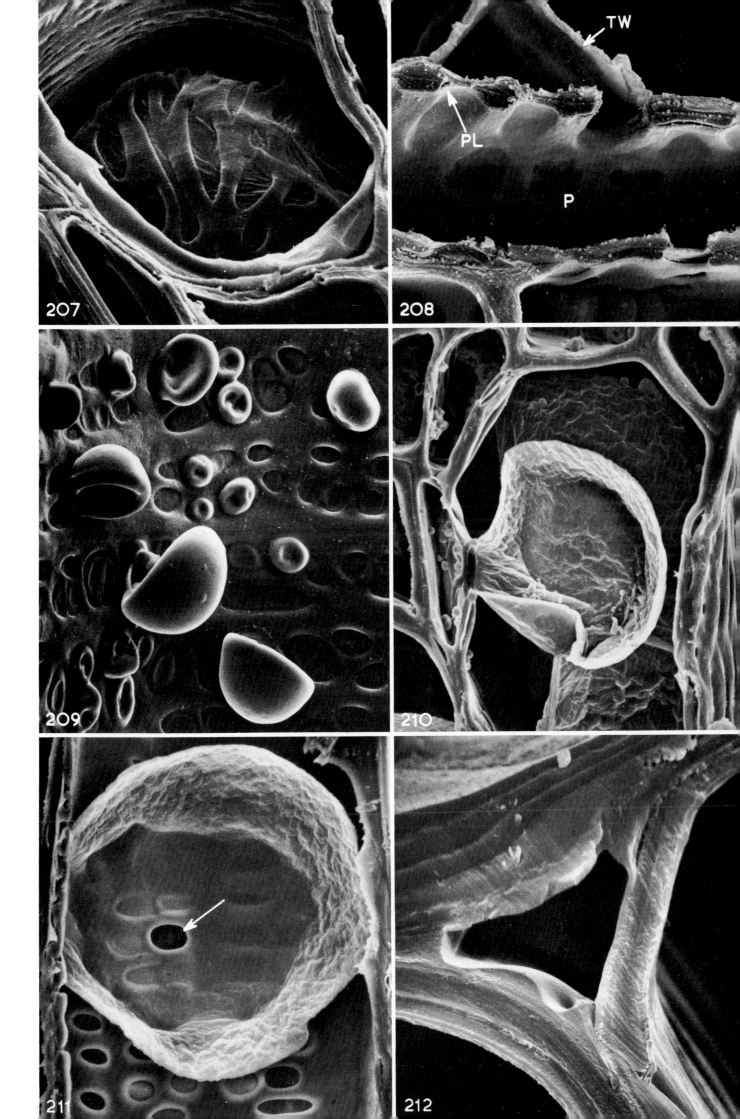

207

208

TW

PL

P

209

210

211

212

differentiate into phloem instead of xylem. These small phloem strands become embedded in the xylem as soon as the cambium resumes its normal bidirectional production of xylem and phloem. Alternatively, in other species, the cessation of small arcs of cambial activity causes the phloem to become sunken into grooves in the surface of the xylem cylinder. When the circular outline of the cambium is restored outside these sunken areas of phloem, strands of included phloem result. *Concentric* strands of included phloem are usually the result of the development of successive cambia [154], each vascular cambium producing xylem to the inside and phloem strands and parenchyma to the outside of the stem.

4.11 Storeyed wood

When wood is viewed in a *radial section* many of the cells often appear to lie in definite layers. This is, of course, a direct consequence of all the derivates of each radial file having been divided off the same fusiform cambial initial and xylem mother cells. Such a stratification is often clearly apparent in tracheids, vessel elements and strands of axial parenchyma cells. Because fibres lengthen by intrusive tip growth during their differentiation, their stratification is less clear. When wood is viewed in *tangential section*, however, the cells of the vascular cambium and its derivates show one of two basic patterns. In all softwoods and most hardwoods the cells are arranged in a more or less irregular pattern with the ends of adjoining cells overlapping (Figs. 130, 131, 218 and 220). Such an arrangement is the consequence of an anticlinal cell division cycle in the cambium, and the fusiform initials and their derivatives are said to be *non-storeyed* [141]. Non-storeyedness is essential for good conductivity between tracheids where the pitting in the side wall provides the main pathway for water from cell to cell. It also contributes to the along the grain strength in softwoods. In some of the more advanced and highly specialized hardwood species, however, the fusiform cambial initials lie in definite horizontal rows or tiers when viewed in the tangential plane [17, 141]. The cells in such an arrangement are said to be *storeyed* (sometimes spelt *storied* in the American literature) and the storeyed nature of the fusiform cambial initials is reflected in the arrangement of vessel elements and axial parenchyma strands derived from them (Figs. 219 and 221). Again, the intrusive growth of the fibres that accompanies their differentiation tends to obliterate any storeyedness in these cells. Storeyedness is associated with the evolution of short, wide, simple-perforated vessel elements where conduction is primarily through an almost transverse end wall and with the evolution of long libriform fibres where considerable extension growth of their tips has produced a strong stem support system. Storeyedness

Fig. 213. Concentric bands of fibres, vessels, and axial parenchyma cells alternating with concentric bands of thin walled parenchyma and included phloem in *Heimerliodendron brunonianum* (Endl.) Skotsb. (Nyctaginaceae). TF × 70.

Fig. 214. Concentric bands of normal wood separated by strands of included phloem (IP) and bands of axial and isodiametric parenchyma (P), and thick walled sclereids (SC) in the wood of *Avicennia resinifera* Forst. f. (Avicenniaceae). This arrangement is a consequence of the development of successive vascular cambia. TF × 150.

Fig. 215. Detail of an included phloem strand (crushed) in *Heimerliodendron brunonianum*. TF × 450.

Fig. 216. Detail of an included phloem strand in *Avicennia resinifera*. TF × 400.

Fig. 217. Detail of included phloem in *Avicennia resinifera* showing sieve tube elements (ST) and companion cells (CC). Note the two incomplete sieve plates (SP). TF × 2200.

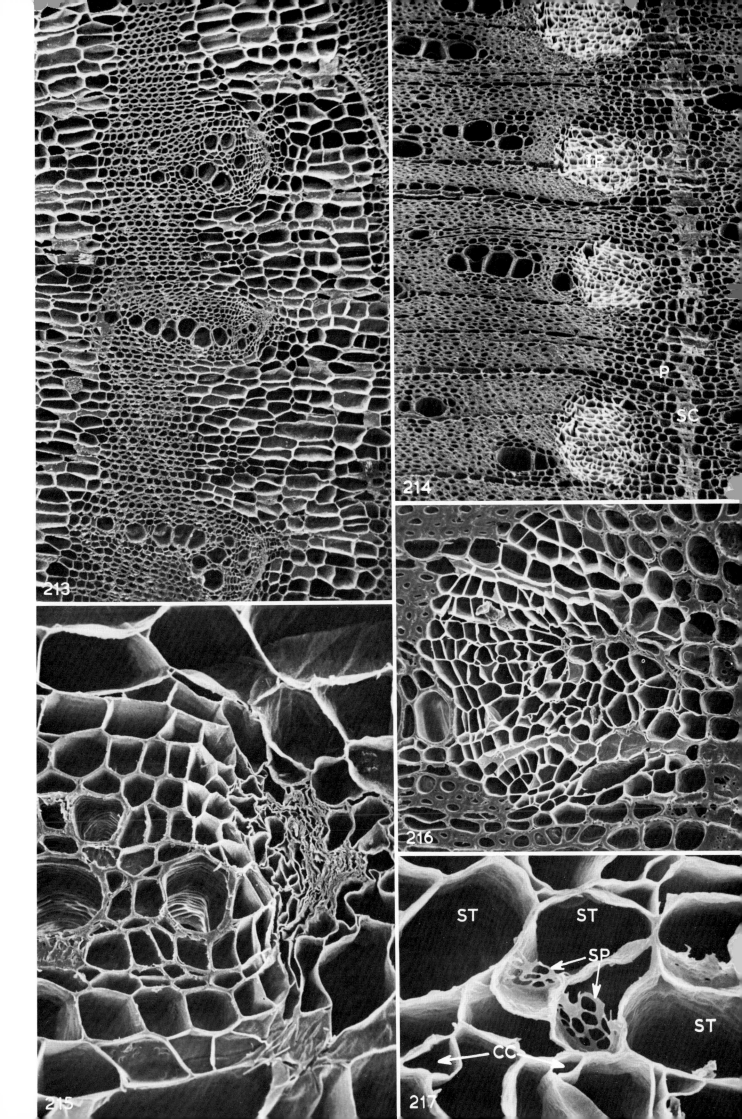

usually becomes more marked with increasing distance from the stem centre.

Some hardwoods have their rays arranged in storeys when viewed in tangential section [75]. Where each ray is only the same height as the neighbouring fusiform initials this effect can appear very striking. In most storeyed woods, however, the rays extend through several storeys of fusiform initials and their derivatives so that the storeyed effect is either lost or less pronounced.

4.12 Tension wood

Tension wood is modified wood found to the upper side of leaning branches and trunks in most hardwoods [143, 177]. It is usually accompanied by an eccentric growth of the stem. Like softwood compression wood (*see* Section 2.8), hardwood tension wood develops as a reaction response to gravity or possibly stress [16] and apparently exerts sufficient force to maintain branches at their predetermined angle.

Tension wood is usually harder and denser than normal wood and is sometimes darker in colour [43]. Its presence can often be detected in sawn timber by the woolly appearance of the cut surface.

Anatomically tension wood can show a variety of differences from the normal wood of the same tree (*see* Figs. 222 and 223). The vessels are usually smaller and more sparsely distributed. In some woods, the fibres are modified by the deposition of a prominent inner wall layer known as the gelatinous layer (Fig. 224). When present, this *gelatinous* or *G-layer* may lie inside the S_3 layer, replace the S_3 layer, replace both the S_2 and S_3, or more rarely lie between the S_2 and S_3 layers in an $S_1 + S_2 + G + S_3$ configuration [40]. The G-layer is an unlignified layer of small-angle cellulose microfibrils, sometimes convoluted on the lumen surface [33] (Fig. 224) and easily separated from the rest of the secondary wall (Figs. 224 and 225). It is built up of concentric lamellae, occasionally appearing to be multi-layered (Fig. 226). Fibres with a G-layer are known as *tension wood fibres* [37] or *gelatinous fibres*. The inner pit apertures in tension wood fibres tend to lie along the long axis of the cell because of the small microfibril angle of the G-layer [138]. Abnormally long pit apertures may develop by the coalescence of a number of these apertures. Tension wood fibres tend to have a higher cellulose content than do fibres from the normal wood of the same species [159]. The higher cellulose content is generally attributed to the presence of the G-layer. Tension wood fibres have a similar lignin content to normal wood fibres but the lignin content is concentrated in their non-gelatinous layers [11]. The S_1 layer is usually slightly more lignified and the S_2 layer almost invariably more lignified than the equivalent secondary wall layer in the normal wood of that species. The degree of lignification

Fig. 218. Tangential, longitudinal face of the non-storeyed wood of *Paratrophis microphylla* (Raoul) Ckn. (Moraceae). TLF × 140.

Fig. 219. Tangential longitudinal face of the storeyed wood of *Corynocarpus laevigatus* J. R. et G. Forst (Corynocarpaceae). Note how the vessel elements and the tapered ends of the paranchyma strands are distinctly stratified. TLF × 140.

Fig. 220. Non-storeyed axial parenchyma strands in *Paratrophis microphylla*. TLF × 475.

Fig. 221. Storeyed axial parenchyma strands in *Corynocarpus laevigatus*. The ends of the parenchyma strands have pointed tips. TLF × 300.

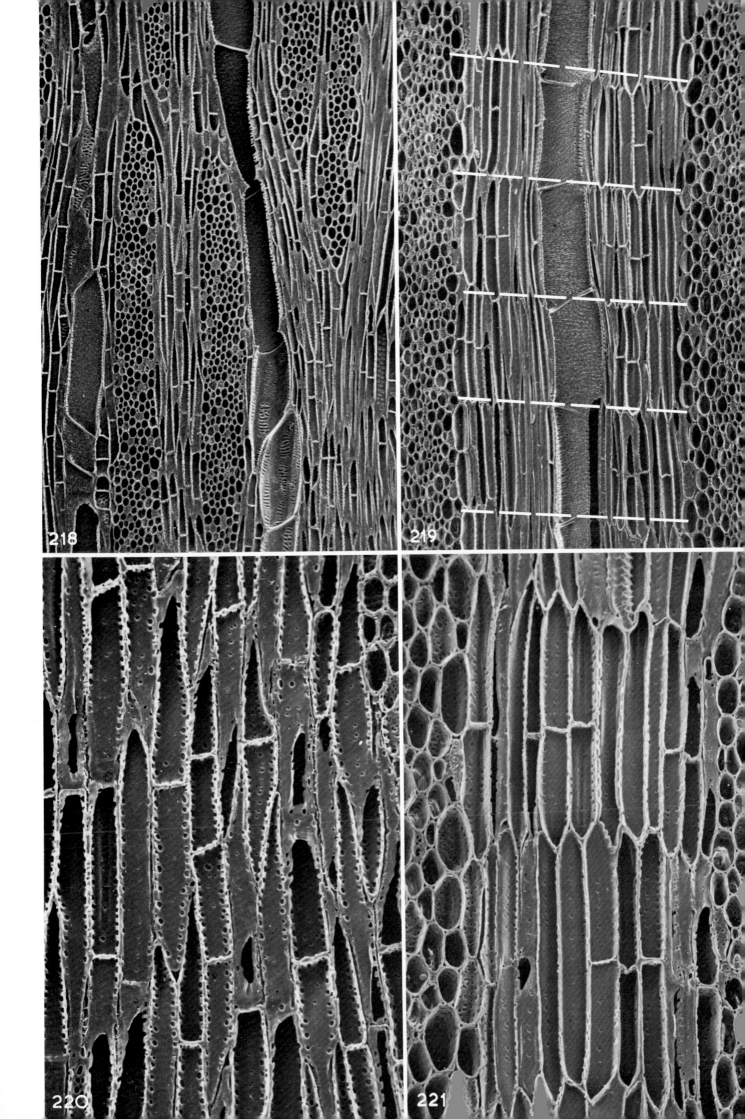

is related to the thickness of the G-layer, with a highly lignified S_2 layer usually being associated with a thin G-layer. Gymnosperm tracheids with a G-layer have occasionally been recorded [67, 74, 159].

Not all hardwoods have tension wood fibres in their tension wood [43, 147, 152]. Instead the fibres may merely show differences in the thickness of their secondary wall accompanied by a reduction in the microfibril angle of the S_2 layer. Hardwoods lacking tension wood fibres may also show greater differences in the distribution of the vessels, fibre and parenchyma between their tension and normal woods than do species with tension wood fibres. In *Entelea aborescens* R.Br. (Tiliaceae), an example of a wood lacking tension wood fibres, the eccentricity to the upper side of the inclined stem is accentuated by a reduction in the bands of thin-walled parenchyma cells found in the otherwise normal wood to the lower side of the stem.

Although the longitudinal shrinkage of tension wood is not as high as that of compression wood, it is nevertheless much higher than that of normal hardwood. This has been attributed to the large microfibril angle of the outer cell wall layers. Although it has a high tensile strength when air dried, tension wood is a serious defect in timber since it may collapse owing to excessive and uneven shrinkage.

It is also worth noting that not all hardwoods have modified or tension wood associated with an eccentric growth to the upper side of the leaning stem. Many vessel-less hardwoods, such as *Pseudowintera* [85] (Winteraceae), have an eccentric growth to the lower side of the inclined branch as in the softwoods. A similar situation exists in leaning stems of the porous wood *Buxus sempervirens* L. (Buxaceae) [68].

Fig. 222. Transverse section through normal wood fibres of *Salix alba* L. (Salicaceae). TF × 1500.

Fig. 223. Transverse section through tension wood fibres of *Salix alba* L. (Salicaceae). Note the presence of the G-layer. TF × 1500.

Fig. 224. Detail of tension wood fibres in *Paratrophis microphylla* (Raoul) Ckn. (Moraceae). The G-layer (arrowed) is loosely attached to the normal secondary wall. TF × 4500.

Fig. 225. Tension wood fibres *Paratrophis microphylla* (Raoul) Ckn. (Moraceae). The G-layer is poorly developed in this particular wood sample and has separated from the secondary wall during specimen cutting. TF × 1250.

Fig. 226. Tension wood fibres with multi-laminate G-layers in *Carmichaelia arborea* (Forst.f.) Druce (Papilionaceae). TF × 2800.

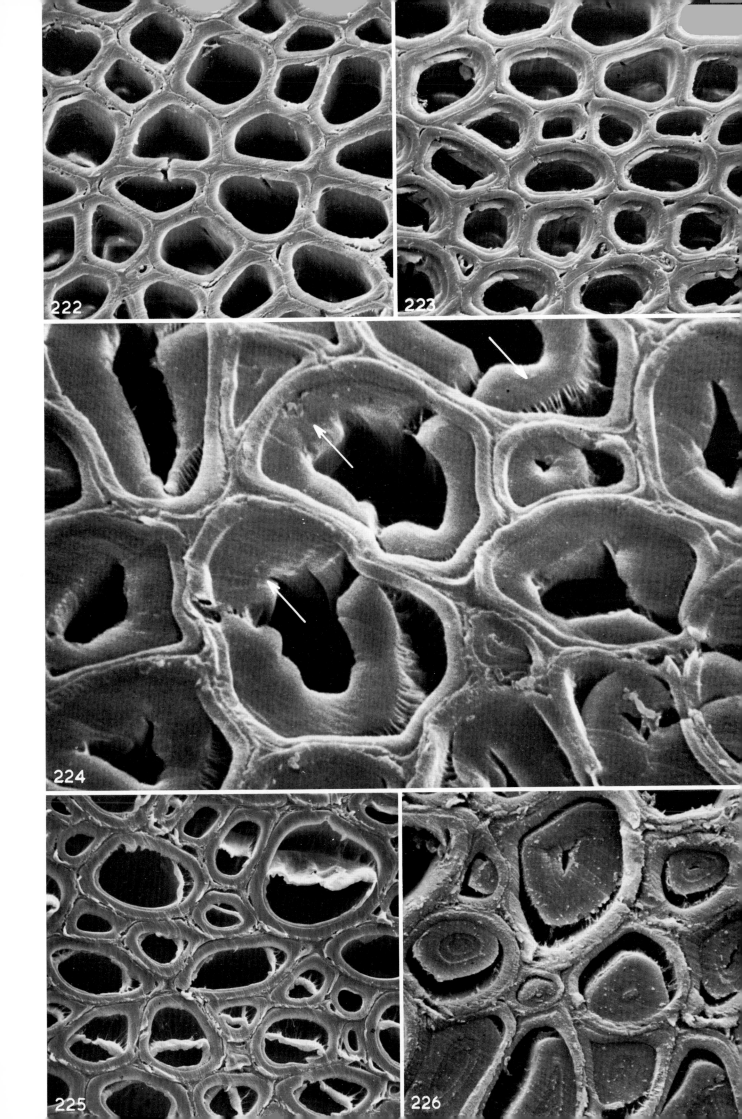

References

[1] Baas, P. (1973), The wood anatomical range in *Ilex* (Aquifoliaceae) and its ecological and phylogenetic significance. *Blumea*, **21**, 193–258.

[2] Baird, W. M. (1974), Development and composition of the warty layer in Balsam Fir (*Abies balsamea*). *Abstract Bulletin of the Institute of Paper Chemistry*, **45**, 3865.

[3] Baird, W. M., Parham, R. A. & Johnson, M. A. (1974), Development and composition of the warty layer in Balsam Fir. I. Development. *Wood and Fiber*, **6**, 114–25.

[4] Baird, W. M., Johnson, M. A. & Parham, R. A. (1974), Development and composition of the warty layer in Balsam Fir. II. Composition. *Wood and Fiber*, **6**, 211–22.

[5] Bamber, R. K. (1976), Tylosoids in the resin canals of the heartwood of some species of Shorea. *Holzforschung*, **30**, 59–62.

[6] Bamber, R. K. (1976), Heartwood, its function and formation. *Wood Science & Technology*, **10**, 1–8.

[7] Bamber, R. K. & Davies, G. W. (1969), Lignification of ray parenchyma cell walls in the wood of *Pinus radiata* D. Don. *Holzforschung*, **23**, 83–4.

[8] Banks, W. B. (1971), Structure of the bordered pit membrane in certain softwoods as seen by scanning electron microscopy. *Journal of the Institute of Wood Science*, **5**, 12–15.

[9] Barnett, J. R. & Harris, J. M. (1975), Early stages of bordered pit formation in Radiata Pine. *Wood Science and Technology*, **9**, 233–41.

[10] Bauch, J., Liese, W. & Schultze, R. (1972), The morphological variability of the bordered pit membranes in gymnosperms. *Wood Science and Technology*, **6**, 165–84.

[11] Bentum, A. L. K. & Côté, W. A. (1969), Distribution of lignin in normal and tension wood. *Wood Science and Technology*, **3**, 218–31.

[12] Berend, J. H. (1976), On the occurrence of silica grains in the secondary xylem of the Chrysobalanceae. *International Association of Wood Anatomists Bulletin*, 1976/2, 19–29.

[13] Bolton, A. J. (1976), Biological implications of a model describing liquid flow through conifer wood. In: *Wood Structure in Biological and Technological Research*. Ed. P. Baas, A. J. Bolton & D. M. Catlin. Leiden Botanical Series, **3**, 222–37.

[14] Bolton, A. J. & Petty, J. A. (1977), Variation in susceptibility to aspiration of bordered pits in conifer wood. *Journal of Experimental Botany*, **28**, 935–41.

[15] Bonnemain, J. L. (1969), Internal and included phloem in the dicotyledons: their histogenesis and physiology. *Revue Generale de Botanique*, **76**, 5–36.

[16] Boyd, J. D. (1977), Basic cause of differentiation of tension wood and compression wood. *Australian Forest Research*, **7**, 121–43.

[17] Butterfield, B. G. (1972), Developmental changes in the vascular cambium of *Aeschonomene hispida* Willd. *New Zealand Journal of Botany*, **10**, 373–86.

[18] Butterfield, B. G. & Meylan, B. A. (1972), Trabeculae in a hardwood. *International Association of Wood Anatomists Bulletin*, 1972/1, 3–9.

[19] Butterfield, B. G. & Meylan, B. A. (1972), Intervessel pit membranes in *Knightia excelsa* R. Br. *International Association of Wood Anatomists Bulletin*, 1972/4, 3–9.

[20] Butterfield, B. G. & Meylan, B. A. (1972), Scalariform perforation plate development in *Laurelia novae-zelandiae* A. Cunn.: A scanning electron microscope study. *Australian Journal of Botany*, **20**, 253–9.

[21] Butterfield, B. G. & Meylan, B. A. (1973), Microfibrillar webs across vessel pit apertures. *Wood and Fiber*, **5**, 69–75.

[22] Butterfield, B. G. & Meylan, B. A. (1974), Vestured scalariform perforation plate openings in *Neomyrtus pedunculata*. *Australian Journal of Botany*, **22**, 425–7.

[23] Butterfield, B. G. & Meylan, B. A. (1974), Vestured vessel and fibre pits in *Persoonia toru* A. Cunn. (Proteaceae). *International Association of Wood Anatomists Bulletin*, 1974/1, 10–13.

[24] Butterfield, B. G. & Meylan, B. A. (1975), Simple to scalariform combination perforation plates in *Vitex lucens* Kirk (Verbenaceae) and *Brachyglottis repanda* J. R. et G. Forst (Compositae). *International Association of Wood Anatomists Bulletin*, 1975/3, 39–42.

[25] Butterfield, B. G. & Meylan, B. A. (1976), The occurrence of septate fibres in some New Zealand woods. *New Zealand Journal of Botany*, **14**, 123–30.

[26] Butterfield, B. G. & Meylan, B. A. (1979), Observations of trabeculae in New Zealand hardwoods. *Wood Science and Technology*, **13**, 59–65.

[27] Carlquist, S. (1975), *Ecological Strategies of Xylem Evolution*. University of California Press, Berkeley, 259 pp.

[28] Carr, S. G. M. & Carr, D. J. (1975), Intercellular pectic strands in parenchyma. Studies of plant cell walls by scanning electron microscopy. *Australian Journal of Botany*, **23**, 95–105.

[29] Casperson, G. (1963), Über die Bildung der Zellwand beim Reaktionsholz. II. Zur Physiologie des Reaktionsholzes. *Holztechnologie*, **4**, 33–7.

[30] Casperson, G. (1965), The anatomy of reaction wood. *Svensk Papperstidning*, **68**, 534–44.

[31] Chafe, S. C. (1974), Cell wall structure in xylem parenchyma of *Cryptomeria*. *Protoplasma*, **81**, 63–76.

[32] Chafe, S. C. (1974), Cell wall formation and protective layer development in the xylem parenchyma of Trembling Aspen. *Protoplasma*, **80**, 335–54.

[33] Chafe, S. C. (1977), Radial dislocations in the fibre wall of *Eucalyptus regnans* trees of high growth stress. *Wood Science and Technology*, **11**, 69–77.

[34] Chafe, S. C. & Chauret, G. (1974), Cell wall structure

in the xylem parenchyma of Trembling Aspen. *Protoplasma*, **80**, 129 – 147.

[35] Clement, A. & Janin, G. (1973), Further study on the presence of $CaCO_3$ crystals in poplar wood. Existence of five zones recognised by their P content. *Annales des Sciences Forestieres*, **30**, 63 – 81.

[36] Collett, B. M. (1970), Scanning electron microscopy: A review and report of research in wood science. *Wood and Fiber*, **2**, 113 – 33.

[37] Core, H. A., Côté, W. A. & Day, A. C. (1979), *Wood Structure and Identification*, 2nd Edn. Syracuse University Press, 169 pp.

[38] Côté, W. A. & Day, A. C. (1962), Vestured pits – fine structure and apparent relationship with warts. *Tappi*, **45**, 906 – 10.

[39] Côté, W. A., Day, A. C. & Timmel, T. E. (1968), Distribution of lignin in normal and compression wood of Tamarack. *Wood Science and Technology*, **2**, 13 – 33.

[40] Côté, W. A., Day, A. C. & Timell, T. E. (1969), A contribution to the ultrastructure of tension wood fibres. *Wood Science and Technology*, **3**, 257 – 71.

[41] Côté, W. A. & Krahmer, R. L. (1962), The permeability of coniferous pits demonstrated by electron microscopy. *Tappi*, **45**, 119 – 22.

[42] Creber, G. T. (1977), Tree rings: a natural data storage system. *Biological Review*, **52**, 349 – 83.

[43] Dadswell, H. E. and Wardrop, A. B. (1949), What is reaction wood? *Australian Forestry*, **13**, 22 – 33.

[44] Dinwoodie, J. M. (1961), Tracheid and fibre length in timber. A review of literature. *Forestry*, **3**, 125 – 44.

[45] Esau, K. (1965), *Plant Anatomy*. 2nd Edn. John Wiley and Son, New York, 767 pp.

[46] Exley, R. R., Butterfield, B. G. & Meylan, B. A. (1973), The preparation of wood specimens for the scanning electron microscope. *Journal of Microscopy*, **101**, 21 – 30.

[47] Exley, R. R., Meylan, B. A. & Butterfield, B. G. (1977), A technique for obtaining clean cut surfaces on wood samples prepared for the scanning electron microscope. *Journal of Microscopy*, **110**, 75 – 8.

[48] Fahn, A. & Leshem, B. (1962), Wood fibres with living protoplasts. *New Phytologist*, **62**, 91 – 9.

[49] Fengel, D. (1972), Structure and function of the membrane in softwood bordered pits. *Holzforschung*, **26**, 1 – 9.

[50] Filin, V. R. (1968), The vestured pits of conifers. *Bulletin Moskovskogo Obscestva Ispytateles Privody*, **73**, 65 – 81.

[51] Foster, R. C. (1967), Fine structure of tyloses in three species of the Myrtaceae. *Australian Journal of Botany*, **15**, 25 – 34.

[52] Frey-Wyssling, A. (1959), *Die pflanzliche Zellwand*. Springer-Verlag, Berlin.

[53] Frey-Wyssling, A. (1976), *The Plant Cell Wall*. Handbook of Plant Anatomie. III.4. Gebrüder Borntraeger, Berlin, 294 pp.

[54] Fujita, M., Kato, M., Saiki, H. & Harada, H. (1975), Changes in parenchyma cell structure followed by incubated tylosis development in *Quercus serrata* Thunb. *Bulletin of the Kyoto University Forests*, **47**, 144 – 51.

[55] Gottwald, H. P. J. (1972), Tyloses in fibre tracheids. *Wood Science and Technology*, **6**, 121 – 27.

[56] Gray, R. L. (1973), Multiseriate rays in redwood (*Sequoia sempervirens* (D. Don) Endl.). *International Association of Wood Anatomists Bulletin*, 1973/1, 7 – 8.

[57] Gray, R. L. & de Zeeuw, C. H. (1974), Terminology for multiperforate plates in vessel elements. *International Association of Wood Anatomists Bulletin*, 1974/2, 22 – 7.

[58] Gregory, S. C. & Petty, J. A. (1973), Valve actions of bordered pits in conifers. *Journal of Experimental Botany*, **24**, 763 – 67.

[59] Hale, J. D. (1923), Trabeculae of Sanio – their origin and distribution. *Science*, **57**, 155.

[60] Hale, J. D. (1951), The structure of wood. In: Canadian woods – their properties and uses. *Forests Products Laboratories Division*, Ottawa, 66.

[61] Harada, H. & Côté, W. A. (1967), Cell wall organisation in the pit border region of softwood tracheids. *Holzforschung*, **21**, 81 – 5.

[62] Harris, J. M. (1977), Shrinkage and density of radiata pine compression wood in relation to its anatomy and mode of formation. *New Zealand Journal of Forest Science*, **7**, 91 – 106.

[63] Hillis, W. E. (1977), Secondary changes in wood. In: *Recent Advances in Phytochemistry*, **11**, *The Structure, Biosynthesis and Degradation of Wood*, Ed. Frank A. Loewus & V. C. Runeckles, Plenum Press, New York, 247 – 309.

[64] Hillis, W. E. & de Silva, D. (1979), Inorganic extraneous constituents of wood. *Holzforschung*, **33**, 47 – 53.

[65] Hirata, T., Saiki, H. & Harada, H. (1972), Observation of crystals and silica inclusions in parenchyma cells of certain tropical woods by scanning electron microscope. *Bulletin of the Kyoto University Forests*, **44**, 194 – 205.

[66] Hodge, A. J. & Wardrop, A. B. (1950), An electron microscope investigation of the cell wall organisation in conifer tracheids and conifer cambium. *Australian Journal of Scientific Research*, **B3**, 265 – 9.

[67] Höster, H. R. (1970), Gelatinose Tracheiden in sekundaren xylem von *Larix leptolepis* (S. & Z.) Gord. *Holzforschung*, **24**, 4 – 6.

[68] Höster, H. R. & Liese, W. (1966), Über das Vorkomemen von Reaktionsgewebe in Wirzeln und Asten der Dikotyledonen. *Holzforschung*, **20**, 80 – 90.

[69] Imamura, Y. & Harada, H. (1973), Electron microscopic study on the development of the bordered pit in coniferous tracheids. *Wood Science and Technology*, **7**, 189 – 205.

[70] Imamura, Y., Harada, H. & Saiki, H. (1974), Further study on the development of the bordered pit in coniferous tracheids. *Journal of the Japan Wood Research Society*, **20**, 157 – 65.

[71] Ishida, S. & Ohtani, J. (1970), Study on the pit of wood cells using scanning electron microscopy. Report 1.

An observation of the vestured pit in black locust, *Robinia pseudoacacia* L. *Research Bulletins of the College of Experimental Forests, Hokkaido,* **27**, 247 – 54.

[72] Ishida, S. & Ohtani, J. (1974), An observation of scalariform perforation plate of the vessel in some hardwoods using scanning electron microscope. *Research Bulletins of the College of Experiment Forests, Hokkaido,* **31**, 79 – 85.

[73] Itoh, T. (1979), Studies of the structure and growth of primary walls of woody plants. *Wood Research Bulletin of the Wood Research Institute, Kyoto University,* **65**, 54 – 110.

[74] Jacquiot, C. & Trenard, Y. (1974), The occurrence of gelatinous tracheids in softwoods. *Holzforschung,* **28**, 73 – 6.

[75] Jane, F. W. (1970), *The Structure of Wood.* 2nd Edn. A. & C. Black, London, 478 pp.

[76] Jutte, S. M. (1977), A wood anatomical contribution to the understanding of vascular wilt disease. *International Association of Wood Anatomists Bulletin* 1977/4, 77 – 81.

[77] Jutte, S. M. & Levy, J. (1973), Helical thickenings in the tracheids of *Taxus & Pseudotsuga* as revealed by the scanning reflection electron microscope. *Acta Botanica Neerlandica,* **22**, 100 – 5.

[78] Kanazawa, K. (1968), Electron microscopic investigation on the vestured pit. *Bulletin of Faculty of Agriculture, Shizuoka University Iwata,* **18**, 75 – 83.

[79] Kishi, K., Harada, H. & Saiki, H. (1977), Layered Structure of the secondary wall in vessels of hardwoods by polarizing microscopy. *Bulletin of Kyoto University Forests,* **49**, 122 – 6.

[80] Kishi, K., Harada, H. & Saiki, H. (1979), An electron microscope study of the layered structure of the secondary wall in vessels. *Journal Japanese Wood Research Society,* **25**, 521 – 7.

[81] Keith, C. T. (1971), Observations on the anatomy and fine structure of the trabeculae of sanio. *International Association of Wood Anatomists Bulletin,* 1971/3, 3 – 11.

[82] Keith, C. T. (1975), Tangential wall thickenings in conifer tracheids at ray-contact areas. *Wood and Fiber,* **7**, 129 – 35.

[83] Kloot, N. H. (1952), Mechanical and physical properties of Coconut Palm. *Australian Journal of Applied Science,* **3**, 293 – 323.

[84] Kucera, L. J., Meylan, B. A. & Butterfield, B. G. (1977), Vestured simple perforation plates. *International Association of Wood Anatomists Bulletin,* 1977/1, 3 – 6.

[85] Kucera, L. J. & Philipson, W. R. (1978), Growth eccentricity and reaction anatomy in branchwood of *Pseudowintera colorata. American Journal of Botany,* **65**, 601 – 7.

[86] Liese, W. (1965), The warty layer. In: *Cellular Ultrastructure of Woody Plants,* Ed. W. A. Côté. Syracuse University Press, 251 – 69.

[87] Liese, W. & Bauch, J. (1967), On the closure of bordered pits in conifers. *Wood Science and Technology,* **1**, 1 – 13.

[88] McGinnes, E. A. & Phelps, J. E. (1972), Intercellular spaces in Eastern Redcedar (*Juniperus virginiana* L.). *Wood Science,* **4**, 225 – 9.

[89] Mann, P. T. (1974), Ray parenchyma cell wall ultrastructure and formation in *Pinus banksiana. Wood and Fiber,* **6**, 18 – 25.

[90] Metcalfe, C. R. & Chalk, L. (1950), *Anatomy of the Dicotyledons.* Volumes 1 and 2. Clarendon Press, Oxford, 1500 pp.

[91] Meyer, R. W. (1967), Tyloses development in white oak. *Forest Products Journal,* **17**, 50 – 56.

[92] Meyer, R. W. & Côté, W. A. (1968), Formation of the protective layer and its role in tylosis development. *Wood Science and Technology,* **2**, 84 – 94.

[93] Meyer, R. W. & Muhammad, A. F. (1971), Scalariform perforation plate fine structure. *Wood and Fiber,* **3**, 139 – 45.

[94] Meylan, B. A. (1978), Density variation within *Cocos nucifera* stems. *New Zealand Journal of Forestry Science,* **8**, 369 – 83.

[95] Meylan, B. A. & Butterfield, B. G. (1972), *Three Dimensional Structure of Wood: A Scanning Electron Microscopy Study.* Chapman and Hall Ltd, London, 80 pp.

[96] Meylan, B. A. & Butterfield, B. G. (1972), Perforation plate development in *Knightia excelsa* R.Br.: a scanning electron microscope study. *Australian Journal of Botany,* **20**, 79 – 86.

[97] Meylan, B. A. & Butterfield, B. G. (1972), Scalariform perforation plates: observations using scanning electron microscopy. *Wood and Fiber,* **4**, 225 – 33.

[98] Meylan, B. A. & Butterfield, B. G. (1973), A trabecula with a vestured pit. *Bulletin of the International Association of Wood Anatomists,* 1973/3, 12 – 14.

[99] Meylan, B. A. & Butterfield, B. G. (1973), Unusual perforation plates: Observations using scanning electron microscopy. *Micron,* **4**, 47 – 59.

[100] Meylan, B. A. & Butterfield, B. G. (1974), Occurrence of vestured pits in the vessels and fibres of New Zealand woods. *New Zealand Journal of Botany,* **12**, 3 – 18.

[101] Meylan, B. A. & Butterfield, B. G. (1975), Occurrence of simple, multiple and combination perforation plates in the vessels of New Zealand woods. *New Zealand Journal of Botany,* **13**, 1 – 18.

[102] Meylan, B. A. & Butterfield, B. G. (1978), Helical orientation of the microfibrils in tracheids, fibres and vessels. *Wood Science and Technology,* **12**, 219 – 22.

[103] Meylan, B. A. & Butterfield, B. G. (1978), Occurrence of helical thickenings in the vessels of New Zealand woods. *New Phytologist,* **81**, 139 – 46.

[104] Meylan, B. A. & Butterfield, B. G. (1978), *The Structure of New Zealand Woods.* New Zealand DSIR Bulletin 222, 250 pp.

[105] Müller-Stoll, von W. R. (1965), Über intrazellulare Stabbildungen (Trabeculae) im Holz als anatomische eigenart bei geholzen exponierter gebirgslagen. In: Metzner, P., Rieth, A., Sagromsky, H. and Stubbe,

H. *Die Kulturpflanze*. *Akademie-Verlag*, Berlin, 763 – 99.

[106] Murmanis, L. (1975), Formation of tyloses in felled *Quercus rubra* L. *Wood Science and Technology*, **9**, 3 – 14.

[107] Murmanis, L. (1976), The protective layer in xylem parenchyma cells of *Quercus rubra* L. *Applied Polymer Symposium*, **28**, 1283 – 92.

[108] Murmanis, L. & Sachs, I. B. (1969), Structure of pit border in *Pinus strobus* L. *Wood and Fiber*, **1**, 7 – 17.

[109] O'Brien, T. P. (1970), Further observations on hydrolysis of the cell wall in the xylem. *Protoplasma*, **69**, 1 – 14.

[110] O'Brien, T. P. & Thimann, K. V. (1967), Observations on the fine structure of the oat coleoptile. III. Correlated light and electron microscopy of the vascular tissues. *Protoplasma*, **63**, 443 – 78.

[111] Oda, K. & Nakasone, H. (1975), Crystals and crystalliferous cells in Okinawan hardwoods. *Science Bulletin of the College of Agriculture, University of the Ryukyus*, **22**, 713 – 20.

[112] Ohtani, J. (1977), An observation of the trabaculae in some dicotyledonous woods using scanning electron microscopy. *Research Bulletins of the College Experimental Forests, Hokkaido University*, **34**, 60 – 74.

[113] Ohtani, J. & Fujikawa, S. (1971), Study of the warty layer by scanning electron microscopy. 1. The variation of warts on the tracheid wall within an annual ring of coniferous woods. *Journal of the Japanese Wood Research Society*, **17**, 89 – 95.

[114] Ohtani, J. & Ishida, S. (1973), An observation of the sculptures of the vessel wall of *Fagus crenata* Bl. using scanning electron microscopy. *Research Bulletins College of Experimental Forests, Hokkaido University*, **30**, 125 – 44.

[115] Ohtani, J. & Ishida, S. (1976), An observation on perforation plate differentiation in *Fagus crenata* Bl. using scanning electron microscopy. *Research Bulletins College Experimental Forests, Hokkaido University*, **33**, 115 – 26.

[116] Ohtani, J. & Ishida, S. (1976), Study on the pit of wood cells using scanning electron microscopy. Report 5. Vestured pits in Japanese dicotyledonous woods. *Research Bulletins College Experimental Forests, Hokkaido University*, **33**, 407 – 36.

[117] Ohtani, J. & Ishida, S. (1978), An observation on the perforation plates in Japanese dicotyledonous woods using scanning electron microscopy. *Research Bulletins College of Experimental Forests, Hokkaido*, **35**, 65 – 116.

[118] Ohtani, J. & Ishida, S. (1978), An observation on the spiral thickenings in the vessel members in Japanese dicotyledonous woods using scanning electron microscopy. *Research Bulletins of the College Experimental Forests, Hokkaido*, **35**, 434 – 64.

[119] Ohtani, J. & Ishida, S. (1978), Pit membrane with torus in dicotyledonous woods. *Journal of the Japanese Wood Research Society*, **24**, 673 – 5.

[120] Orman, H. R. (1974), Strength properties of coconut palm timber. *NZ Forest Research Institute, Timber Engineering Report 1*.

[121] Page, D. H. (1976), A note on the cell wall structure of softwood tracheids. *Wood and Fiber*, **7**, 246 – 8.

[122] Panshin, A. J. & de Zeeuw, C. (1970), *Textbook of Wood Technology*. Volume 1. Third Edn. McGraw-Hill, New York. 705 pp.

[123] Parameswaran, N. & Liese, W. (1969), On the formation and fine structure of septate fibres of *Ribes sanguineum*. *Wood Science and Technology*, **3**, 272 – 86.

[124] Parameswaran, N. & Liese, W. (1973), Scanning electron microscopy of multiperforation perforation plates. *Holzforschung*, **27**, 181 – 86.

[125] Parameswaran, N. & Liese, W. (1974), Vestured pits in vessels and tracheids of *Gnetum*. *International Association of Wood Anatomists Bulletin*, 1974/4, 3 – 7.

[126] Parameswaran, N. & Liese, W. (1976), On the fine structure of bamboo fibres. *Wood Science and Technology*, **10**, 231 – 46.

[127] Parham, R. A. (1973), On the substructure of scalariform perforation plates. *Wood and Fiber*, **4**, 342 – 6.

[128] Parham, R. A. & Baird, W. M. (1973), The bordered pit membrane in differentiating Balsam Fir. *Wood and Fiber*, **5**, 80 – 6.

[129] Parham, R. A. & Baird, W. A. (1974), Warts in the evolution of angiosperm wood. *Wood Science and Technology*, **8**, 1 – 10.

[130] Parham, R. A. & Côté, W. A. (1971), Distribution of lignin in normal and compression wood of *Pinus taeda* L. *Wood Science and Technology*, **5**, 49 – 62.

[131] Parham, R. A. & Kaustinen, H. (1973), On the morphology of spiral thickenings. *International Association of Wood Anatomists Bulletin*, 1973/2, 8 – 17.

[132] Parthasarathy, M. V. (1974), Ultrastructure of phloem in palms. I. Immature sieve elements and parenchymatic elements. *Protoplasma*, **79**, 59 – 91.

[133] Parthasarathy, M. V. (1974), Ultrastructure of phloem in palms. II. Structural changes and fate of the organelles in differentiating sieve elements. *Protoplasma*, **79**, 93 – 125.

[134] Parthasarathy, M. V. (1974), Ultrastructure of phloem in palms. III. Mature phloem. *Protoplasma*, **79**, 295 – 315.

[135] Parthasarathy, M. V. & Klotz, L. H. (1976), Palm 'wood'. I. Anatomical aspects. *Wood Science and Technology*, **10**, 215 – 29.

[136] Parthasarathy, M. V. & Klotz, L. H. (1976), Palm 'wood'. II. Ultrastructural aspects of sieve elements, tracheary elements and fibres. *Wood Science and Technology*, **10**, 247 – 71.

[137] Parathasarathy, M. V. & Tomlinson, P. B. (1967), Anatomical features of metaphloem in stems of sabal, cocos and two other palms. *American Journal of Botany*, **54**, 1143 – 51.

[138] Patel, R. N. (1962), On the occurrence of gelatinous fibres with special reference to root wood. M.Sc. thesis, University of London.

[139] Peters, W. J. (1974), Tylosis formation in *Pinus* tracheids. *Botanical Gazette*, **135**, 126 – 31.

[140] Petty, J. A. (1971), The aspiration of bordered pits in conifer wood. *Proceedings of the Royal Society London, B*, **181**, 395 – 406.

[141] Philipson, W. R., Ward, J. M., & Butterfield, B. G. (1971), *The Vascular Cambium: Its Development and Activity*. Chapman and Hall, London, 182 pp.

[142] Preston, R. D. (1974), *The Physical Biology of Plant Cell Walls*. Chapman and Hall, London, 491 pp.

[143] Robards, A. W. (1969), The effect of gravity on the formation of wood. *Science Progress*, **57**, 513 – 32.

[144] Ruel, K., Barnard, F. & Goring, D. A. I. (1978), Lamellation in the S2 layer of softwood tracheids as demonstrated by scanning transmission electron microscopy. *Wood Science and Technology*, **12**, 287 – 291.

[145] Sachs, I., Kuntz, J., Ward, J., Nair, G. & Schultz, N. (1970), Tyloses structure. *Wood and Fiber*, **2**, 259 – 68.

[146] Schmid, R. & Machado, R. D. (1964), Zur entstehung und feinstruker skulpturierter Hoftupfel bei Leguminosen. *Planta*, **60**, 612 – 26.

[147] Scurfield, G. (1964), The nature of reaction wood. IX. Anomolous cases of reaction anatomy. *Australian Journal of Botany*, **12**, 173 – 84.

[148] Scurfield, G., Anderson, C. A. & Segnit, E. R. (1974), Silica in woody stems. *Australian Journal of Botany*, **22**, 211 – 29.

[149] Scurfield, G., Michel, A. J. & Silva, S. R. (1973), Crystals in woody stems. *Botanical Journal of the Linnean Society*, **66**, 277 – 89.

[150] Scurfield, G. & Silva, S. R. (1970), The vestured pits in *Eucalyptus regnans* F. Muell: a study using scanning electron microscopy. *Botanical Journal of the Linnean Society London*, **63**, 313 – 20.

[151] Scurfield, G., Silva, S. R. & Ingle, H. O. (1970), Vessel wall structure: an investigation using scanning electron microscopy. *Australian Journal of Botany*, **18**, 301 – 12.

[152] Scurfield, G. & Wardrop, A. B. (1962), The nature of reaction wood. VI. The reaction anatomy of seedlings of woody perenials. *Australian Journal of Botany*, **10**, 93 – 105.

[153] Sebastian, L. P. & Sastry, C. B. R. (1974), Vessel closures in Sugar Maple. *Wood Science*, **6**, 237 – 44.

[154] Studholme, W. P. & Philipson, W. R. (1966), A comparison of the cambium in two woods with included phloem: *Heimerliodendron brunonianum* (Endl.) Stottsb. and *Avicennia resinifera* Forst. f. *New Zealand Journal of Botany*, **4**, 355 – 65.

[155] Takiya, K., Harada, H. & Saiki, H. (1976), The formation of the wart structure in conifer tracheids. *Bulletin of the Kyoto University Forests*, **48**, 187 – 191.

[156] Thomas, R. J. (1968), The development and ultrastructure of the bordered pit membrane in the Southern Yellow Pines. *Holzforschung*, **22**, 38 – 44.

[157] Thomas, R. J. (1972), The ultrastructure of differentiating and mature bordered pit membranes from cypress (*Taxodium distichum* L. Rich). *Wood and Fiber*, **4**, 87 – 94.

[158] Thomas, R. J. & Bonner, L. D. (1974), The ultrastructure of intercellular passageways in vessels of yellow poplar (*Liriodendron tulipifera* L.). Part II. Scalariform performation plates. *Wood Science*, **6**, 193 – 199.

[159] Timell, T. E. (1969), The chemical composition of tension wood. *Svensk Papperstidning*, **72**, 173 – 81.

[160] Timell, T. E. (1973), Ultrastructure of the dormant and active cambial zones and the dormant phloem associated with formation of normal and compression woods in *Picea abies* (L.) Karst. *Technical Publication no. 96, State University of New York College of Environmental Science and Forestry*, Syracuse, New York, 94 pp.

[161] Timell, T. E. (1978), Helical thickenings and helical cavities in normal and compression woods of *Taxus baccata*. *Wood Science and Technology*, **12**, 1 – 15.

[162] Timell, T. E. (1978), Ultrastructure of compression wood in *Ginkgo biloba*. *Wood Science and Technology*, **12**, 89 – 103.

[163] Tomlinson, P. B. & Zimmerman, N. H. (1967), The ''wood'' of monocotyledons. *International Association of Wood Anatomists Bulletin*, 1967/2, 4 – 24.

[164] Van der Graaf, N. A. & Baas, P. (1974), Wood anatomical variation in relation to latitude and altitude. *Blumea*, **22**, 101 – 21.

[165] Van Vliet, G. J. C. M. (1976), Radial vessels in rays. *International Association of Wood Anatomists Bulletin*, 1976/**3**, 35 – 7.

[166] Van Vliet, G. J. C. M. (1978), Vestured pits of Combretacece and allied families. *Acta Botanica Nederlandica*, **27**, 273 – 85.

[167] Wardrop, A. B. (1964), The structure and formation of the cell wall in xylem. In: *Formation of wood in forest trees*, Ed. M. H. Zimmerman, Academic Press, New York, 87 – 134.

[168] Wardrop, A. B. (1965), Cellular differentiation in xylem. In: *Cellular Ultrastructure of Woody Plants*, Ed. W. A. Côté, Syracuse University Press, 61 – 97.

[169] Wardrop, A. B. & Dadswell, H. E. (1951), Helical thickenings and micellar orientation in the secondary wall of conifer tracheids. *Nature*, **168**, 610 – 2.

[170] Wardrop, A. B., Ingle, H. D. & Davies, G. W. (1968), Nature of vestured pits in angiosperms. *Nature*, **197**, 202 – 3.

[171] Wardrop, A. B., Liese, W. & Davies, G. W. (1959), The nature of the wart structure in conifer tracheids. *Holzforschung*, **13**, 115 – 20.

[172] Welle, B. J. H. Ter. (1976), Silica grains in woody plants of the neotropics, especially surinam. In: *Wood Structure in Biological and Technological Research*, Ed. Baas, P., Bolton, A. J. and Catling, D. M. *Leiden Botanical Series*, **3**, 107 – 42.

[173] Welle, B. J. H. Ter. (1975), Spiral thickenings in the axial parenchyma of Chrysobalanaceae. *Acta Botanica Neerlandica*, **24**, 397 – 405.

[174] Welle, B. J. H. Ter. (1976), On the occurrence of silica grains in the secondary xylem of the chrysobalanceae. *International Association of Wood Anatomists Bulletin*, 1976/2, 19 – 29.

[175] Wenham, M. W. & Cusick, R. (1975), The growth

of secondary wood fibres. *New Phytologist*, **74**, 247 – 61.

[176] Wergin, W. & Casperson, G. (1961), Über Enststehung und Aufbau von Reaktionsholzellen. 2. Mitt. Morphologie der Druckholzellen von *Taxus baccata* L. *Holzforschung*, **15**, 44 – 9.

[177] White, D. J. B. (1965), The anatomy of reaction tissues in plants. In: *Viewpoints in Biology IV*. Ed. J. D. Carthy and C. L. Duggington, Butterworth, London, 54 – 82.

[178] Wolkinger, F. (1969), Morphologie und systematische Verbreitung der lebenden Holzfasern bei Sträuchern und Baumen. I. Zur Morphologie und Zytologie. *Holzforschung*, **23**, 135 – 44.

[179] Wolkinger, F. (1971), Morphologie und systematische Verbreitung der lebenden Holzfasern bei Sträuchern und Baumen. III. Systematische Verbreitung und Bäumen. *Holzforschung*, **25**, 29 – 30.

[180] Yamanaka, K. & Harada, H. (1968), The ultrastructure of vessel wall in certain species of Dipterocarpaceae wood. *Bulletin Kyoto University Forest*, **40**, 293 – 300.

[181] Yata, S., Itoh, T. & Kishima, T. (1970), Formation of perforation plates and bordered pits in differentiated vessel elements. *Wood Research*, **50**, 1 – 11.

[182] Zimmerman, M. H. & Tomlinson, P. B. (1965), Anatomy of the palm *Rhapis excelsa*. I. Mature vegetative axis. *Journal Arnold Arboretum*, **46**, 160 – 78.

[183] Zimmerman, M. H. & Tomlinson, P. B. (1972), The vascular system of monocotyledonous stems. *Botanical Gazette*, **133**, 141 – 55.

[184] Zweypfennign, R. G. V. J. (1978), A hypothesis on the function of vestured pits. *International Association of Wood Anatomists Bulletin* 1978/1, 13 – 15.

Index

Numbers in bold type refer to figures

Resin, 24, **52**
  cells, 42
  intercellular, 42
  intracellular, 42
  plates, 24, 42, **94**, **95**
Resin canals, 24, 42
  axial, 44, **52**, **53**, **92**, **97**
  radial, 44, **53**, **87**, **98**
  traumatic, 44
Ring porous wood, 58, **133**

Salix alba,
  alternate intervessel pitting in, **159**
  contact cells in, **201**
  fibres in, **222**
  tension wood in, **223**
Sapwood, definition, 8
Sclereids, 86, **214**
Schefflera digitata,
  multiseriate rays in, **191**
Secondary cell wall, 8
Semi diffuse-porous wood, 58
Semi ring-porous wood, 58, **134**
Septate fibres, 72, **173–177**
Sequoia sempervirens,
  axial parenchyma cells in, **91**
  part biseriate ray in, **81**
  trabeculae in, **38**
Sheath cells, 80, **199**
Sieve elements, 50
Sieve plates, compound (*see* Phloem), 54,
  122, **217**
Silica grains, 24, **50**
Softwood, 6, 28

Sophora microphylla,
  helical thickenings in, **36**
Sophora tetraptera,
  vessel distribution in, **167**
Spiral thickenings (*see* Helical thickenings)
Spring wood, definition, 8
Starch grains, 24, **49**, **58**, **59**, **173**
Stegmata, 50
Storeyed wood, 88, **219**, **221**
Strand tracheids, 42, **92**, **93**
Summerwood, definition, 8

Taxodium distichum,
  intertracheid pits in, **68**
Taxus baccata,
  compression wood in, **103**
  helical thickenings in, **76**
Tectona grandis,
  coalescent pit apertures in, **15**
  fibres in, **168**
Tension wood, 90, **223–226**
  gelatinous fibres, 90
  tension wood fibres, 90, **223–226**
Tertiary wall layer, 9
Tile cells, 82
Torus (*see* Pit)
Trabeculae, 20, **38–41**, **92**
Tracheids, 34, **53**, **54**, **61–66**
Tracheid wall thickenings, 38, **33**, **75**,
  76, **78**, **103**, **104**
Tyloses, 50, 84, **119**, **120**, **204–212**
  pits in, 50, 86, **119**, **120**, **207**

Upright ray cells, 80, **192**, **197**, **199**

Ulmus procera,
  vessel distribution in, **134**

Vasicentric tracheids, 68
Vascular bundles in palm stems, 48,
  105–110
Vascular cambium, 1, 20, 34, 48, 80, 88,
  214
Vascular tracheids, 56, 68
Vessel distribution, 58
  diffuse, 58, **132**
  pore clusters, 58, **137**, **167**, **184**
  pore multiples 58, **136**, **137**
  radial files, 58, **136**
  ring porous, 58, **133**
  semi-ring porous, 58, **134**
  solitary, 58, **135**
  tangential festoons, 58, **138**
Vessel perforations (*see* Perforation
  plates)
Vessel pitting, 66, **159–166**
Vessel-less dicots, 58, **131**
Vestured perforation plates, 66, **156**,
  157
Vestured pits, 14, 66, 68, **19–27**, **163**,
  164, **200**

Wall sculpturing, 16, **28–37**, **75–78**,
  85, **86**
Wall splits, **77**
Warts, 9, 14
Warty layer, 9, 34, **9**, **23**, **63**, **78**
Wood parenchyma (*see* Axial paren-
  chyma)